DETAIL Practice

Building with Steel

Details
Principles
Examples

Alexander Reichel
Peter Ackermann
Alexander Hentschel
Anette Hochberg

Birkhäuser

Edition Detail

Authors:
Alexander Reichel, Dipl.-Ing. Architect, Kassel
Alexander Hentschel, Dr.-Ing., Nuremberg
Peter Ackermann, Dipl.-Ing. Architect, Munich
Anette Hochberg, Dipl.-Ing. Architect, Griesheim

Project manager:
Andrea Wiegelmann, Dipl.-Ing.

Editors:
Nicola Kollmann, Dipl.-Ing. (FH); Christina Schulz, Dipl.-Ing. Architect

Drawings:
Silvia Hollmann, Claudia Hupfloher, Nicola Kollmann, Elisabeth Krammer, Daniel Hajduk, Andrea Saiko,
Dirk Hennig, Gerald Schnell

German–English translation:
Gerd H. Söffker, Philip Thrift, Hannover

©2007 Institut für internationale Architektur-Dokumentation GmbH & Co. KG, Munich
An Edition DETAIL book

ISBN 978-3-7643-8386-2

Printed on acid-free paper made from cellulose bleached without the use of chlorine.

Typesetting & production:
Peter Gensmantel, Andrea Linke, Roswitha Siegler, Simone Soesters

Printed by:
Aumüller Druck, Regensburg

This book is also available in a German language edition (ISBN 978-3-920034-16-4)

A CIP catalogue record for this book is available from the Library of Congress, Washington D.C., USA.

Bibliographic information published by Die Deutsche Bibliothek
Die Deutsche Bibliothek lists this publication in the Deutsche Nationalbibliographie;
detailed bibliographic data is available on the internet at http://dnb.ddb.de.

Institut für internationale
Architektur-Dokumentation GmbH & Co. KG
Sonnenstr. 17, 80331 Munich, Germany
Tel.: +49 89 381620-0
Fax: +49 89 398670
www.detail.de

Distribution Partner:
Birkhäuser – Publishers for Architecture
PO Box 133, 4010 Basel, Switzerland
Tel.: +41 61 2050707
Fax: +41 61 2050792
e-mail: sales@birkhauser.ch
www.birkhauser.ch

DETAIL Practice
Building with Steel

Contents

Introduction

Alexander Reichel

The book is divided into four main sections supplemented by case studies, tables and an index. The order of the chapters extends from examples of complex applications through the jointing and arrangement of the loadbearing structure, the design of structures and, finally, individual products and semi-finished articles made from steel. To start with, two typical structural steelwork projects are presented as examples together with their specific details. Construction and architecture, loadbearing structure and enclosing envelope, are brought together in the drawings, corresponding to the typical working details of architects.

The second part of the book deals with the principles of structural steelwork design and the stability of the various construction elements. This is followed by the fundamentals behind the design of the connections between individual construction elements, which are supplemented by case studies.

A systematic selection of the most important steel sections and semi-finished products rounds off the overview of this subject. This section of the book is complemented by brief explanations of the technical parameters of corrosion and fire protection, thermal and acoustic insulation. Finally, this introduction to structural steelwork includes case studies of steel structures, which demonstrate the diverse range of potential applications, plus tables and data that furnish the reader with a rapid, clear understanding of this subject.

The selection of structures and surface finishes, the delicate design and the profiling of the loadbearing structure, also the layout and precision of the connections, characterise structural steelwork and result in the architectural and sensual appeal of steel structures. The properties of the material initially permit all design freedoms, something that is proved by the diverse architecture of the different structures. Owing to the rapidity of erection, the long economic spans and the relative ease and flexibility with which steel structures can be built, steel is an industrial building material. However, the growth in the number of refurbishment projects and the changing demands regarding interior design open up further application options for structural steelwork.

The combined planning discipline of architects and engineers will thus enable the qualities of this material to come to the fore and steer the diversity of the constructions and semi-finished products in creative directions.

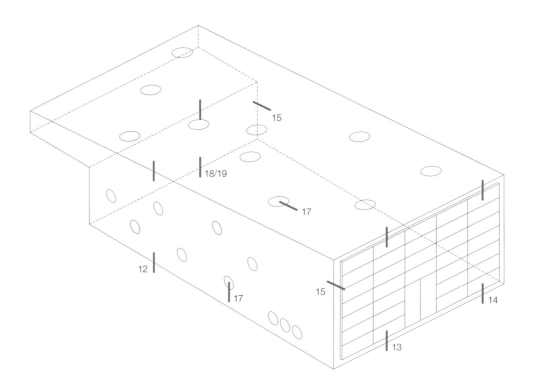

Overview of details
scale 1:20

12   Section through metal facade
      Corner and base of portal frame
13   Section through mezzanine floor
14   Section through glass facade
15   Horizontal section through metal
      and glass facades
16   Composite floor, window strip
17   Rooflight
18   Overhead door
19   Folding door

The demands placed on speed of fabrication and erection, on flexible usage and conversion, plus economic considerations, frequently result in steel being chosen for the loadbearing structures of wide-span industrial sheds.

Example A therefore shows a single-storey shed which could be used as a workshop, warehouse, retail outlet or production plant. The arrangement of the plot corresponds to the layout often found on industrial estates, with circulation around the building possible as well as entrance and exit. The building itself is designed as a compact enclosing envelope offering various types of interior qualities: at the front, reception and display areas plus staff facilities, including changing rooms, and above these further offices which permit direct communication with the main part of the building behind. Between these and the covered loading/unloading area at the rear of the building lie the large open bays devoid of disturbing intervening columns.

Steel permits virtually any shape and size of single-storey shed to be built. Such sheds can be classified according to number of bays, type of roof, the internal structures, overhead cranes, shelving systems, etc. The shed shown here is a single-bay standard structure without overhead crane but including a mezzanine floor for the offices.

The grid of the loadbearing construction in this example is 5 m, a common dimension for such buildings. Such grids have also proved economic, for the sizes of interior furnishings and fittings. A balance has to be found between the depths of floors and beams and the unsupported spans of the sheet metal roof covering, as well as erection options.

In contrast to the offices, the heating to the main part of the shed is minimal (approx. 16°C) – customary these days. The floor area of the open part of the shed is an important criterion because it is this area that determines the applicability of the various standards. For example, in the Industrial Buildings Directive and DIN 18230 the fire protection requirements for sheds up to 200 m^2 are less stringent.

The examples show, primarily, the interaction of loadbearing structure, interior fittings, envelope and architectural ideas. The aim is to explain how a building with an appealing external appearance is developed from a steel loadbearing structure using the jointing logic and lucid geometry of structural steelwork.

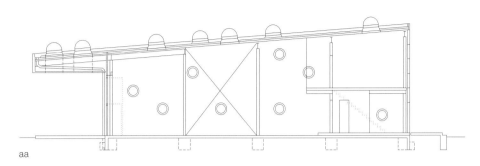

aa

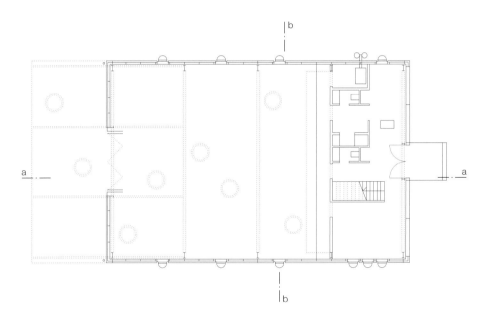

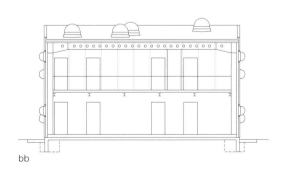

bb

The design of a steel structure is essentially determined by two main features: the loadbearing elements and the external envelope. A steel structure is resolved into individual loadbearing members and therefore is usually designed as a frame.

The loadbearing structure of a building is made up of the foundations, columns, beams, frames, arches or cables forming the loadbearing framework, plus the necessary bracing and stabilising elements.

A loadbearing structure must be stable in at least three directions. The vertical loads to be carried include self-weight, dead, wind, snow and imposed loads. The horizontal loads consist of wind, crane and impact loads. In industrial sheds the type of use means that the risk of impact (by vehicles or cranes) is considerably higher than in conventional buildings. Protection against impact can take the form of using heavier members for the loadbearing construction itself, or the provision of separate barriers.

The loadbearing construction is normally divided into primary and secondary structures. In this example the portal frames and the cantilevering canopy constitute the primary structure, while the trapezoidal sheeting forms the secondary structure. The supporting framework for the envelope is frequently attached to the loadbearing structure, and in this case as the trapezoidal sheeting spans unsupported between the main loadbearing members, this is indeed the secondary structure.

The vertical and horizontal loads are carried on the portal frames. Wind girders in the form of X-bracing in the roof and walls transfer the wind loads down to the foundations. Rails at eaves level and struts between the portal frames complete the bracing effect. Owing to their simple fabrication and erection, portal frames are among the most economic types of structure for short to medium spans, and are very popular. However, they are not suitable for every building form.

A ground slab, pad foundations and a peripheral stem wall as protection against frost heave form the foundations, which transfer the loads from the portal frames into the subsoil.

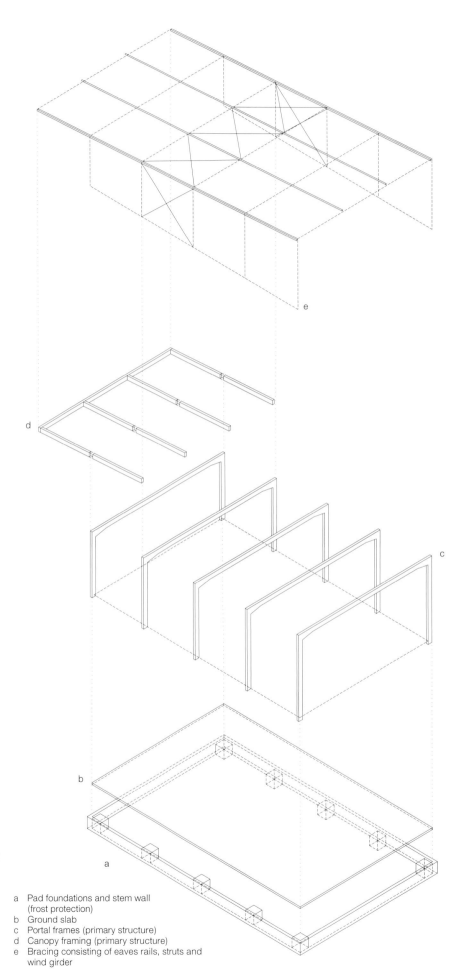

a   Pad foundations and stem wall
    (frost protection)
b   Ground slab
c   Portal frames (primary structure)
d   Canopy framing (primary structure)
e   Bracing consisting of eaves rails, struts and
    wind girder

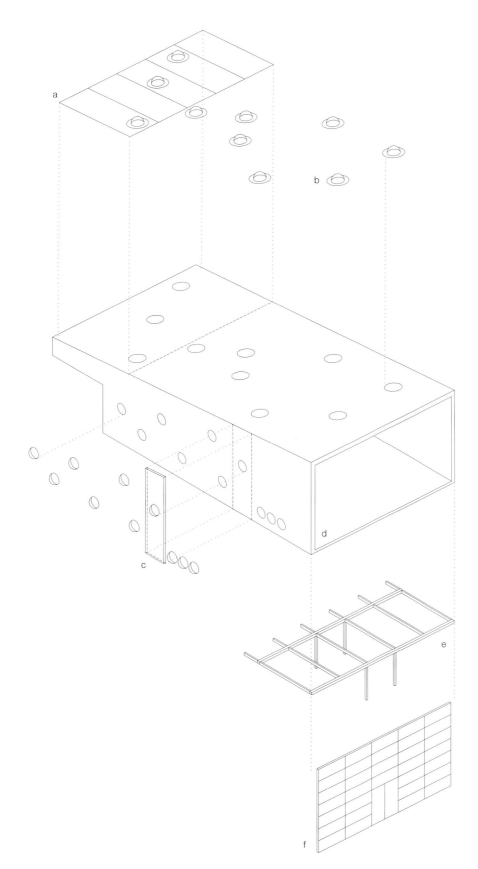

The enclosing envelope to the shed determines the external appearance. The front facade with the entrance is designed as a huge display window, with the necessary functions incorporated into the design. Whereas the canopy at the rear of the building indicates clearly the loading/unloading zone, the sloping roof is a simple way of creating an effective fall for rainwater and also permits a two-storey arrangement at the front (offices) end. Rainwater is collected in a gutter at the rear end of the roof and drained away via downpipes positioned within the envelope. Lighting, ventilation and smoke/heat dissipation requirements are handled by standard rooflights built into the roof (and the side walls!). Their striking layout can be used by the building owner as a simple advertising motif.
The height of the portal frame primary structure decreases towards the rear of the building. The mezzanine floor is simply suspended between the front two portal frames so that the volume of the building can be reduced.

The vertical walls of the external envelope consist of large-format, lightweight panels, so-called sandwich panels. Such elements enable a shed to be enclosed and thermally insulated quickly, economically and without the need for an elaborate supporting framework.
Uninsulated shed walls generally consist of trapezoidal profile sheeting, corrugated sheets or other profiled sheet metal formats. If condensation has to be avoided internally, insulated steel pans, sandwich elements or an insulated facade construction with an air cavity can be employed. Masonry, autoclaved aerated concrete or timber boards can also be used to construct the walls, with or without insulation.

The roof, the horizontal part of the envelope, is designed as an insulated diaphragm. If designed without a slope, such roofs can also carry rooftop planting, which provides ecological and building performance benefits, but introduces additional loads which have an effect on the construction and hence the costs. Clipped sheet metal coverings or sandwich elements represent economic alternatives. Both require a minimum fall.

a   Trapezoidal profile metal sheets
b   Rooflights (also in the walls)
c   Sandwich panel with rooflight
d   Complete envelope
e   Framing to mezzanine floor (secondary structure)
f   Glass facade

Example A
Section through metal facade, frame

□ a

The columns and beams of a portal frame
are rigidly connected at the corners. The
column is normally called a leg, and the
beam a cross-beam or rafter. All the internal forces are transferred across this connection. In the case of I-section members,
the axial force is carried by the entire
cross-section, the shear by the web and
the bending by the flanges. In order to
accommodate the bending moment in
the cross-beam due to the deflection,
haunched ends (as shown here) can be
incorporated. The haunch increases the
lever arm at the end plates and the geometric arrangement of the sections (equal
widths) can thus be maintained. In very
economic connections, the end plates for
transferring the forces frequently extend
beyond the actual section itself. This is a
pragmatic form of connection but is less
convincing in terms of its architecture and
requires very careful detailing of the subsequent layers (roof construction, thermal
insulation, waterproofing) at this point.
Circular holes are cut (flame or laser) in
each cross-beam to ease the routing of
services through the building.

□ b

The foundations carry the vertical and
horizontal loads transferred from the portal frames. A pocket to accommodate a
shear connector and threaded bars are
cast into each pad foundation. The shear
connector, normally a steel section welded
to the underside of the baseplate, resists
the horizontal shear. The pre-assembled
portal frames are erected, levelled with
the help of shims under the baseplates
and then bolted down. This arrangement
compensates for the inevitable inaccuracies in the concrete foundations. The
pocket and the gap beneath the baseplate are then filled with grout. This leg
baseplate detail typical of industrial
sheds is an economic way of transferring
the loads from the portal frame to the
foundation. Although this simple connection looks like a fixed base, the thickness
and stiffness of the baseplate plus the
arrangement of the holding-down bolts
determine whether the base has been
designed as fixed or pinned. The stem
wall to prevent frost heave is a precast
concrete component that is placed on the
foundation and secured with dowels. It
serves as permanent formwork for the
edge of the ground slab. In order to avoid
interrupting the external finishes, there is
a step in each concrete pad foundation
on the outside.

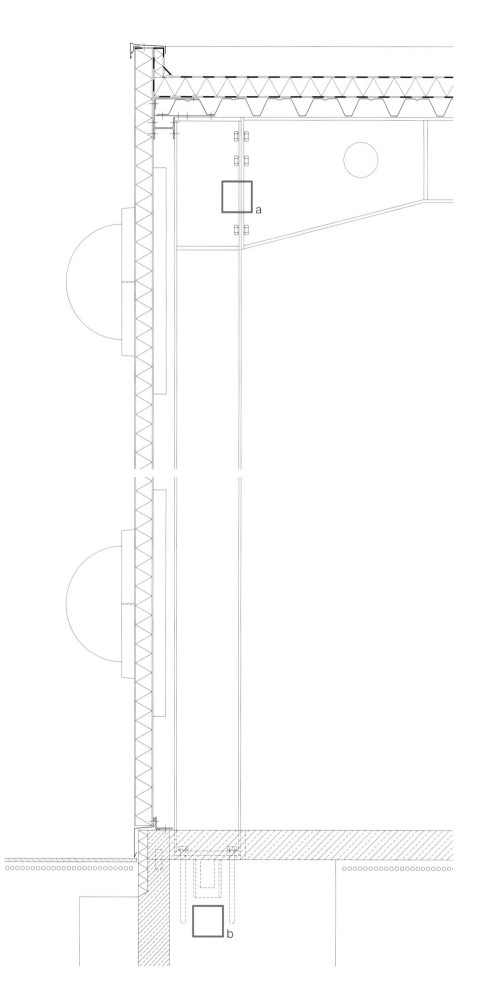

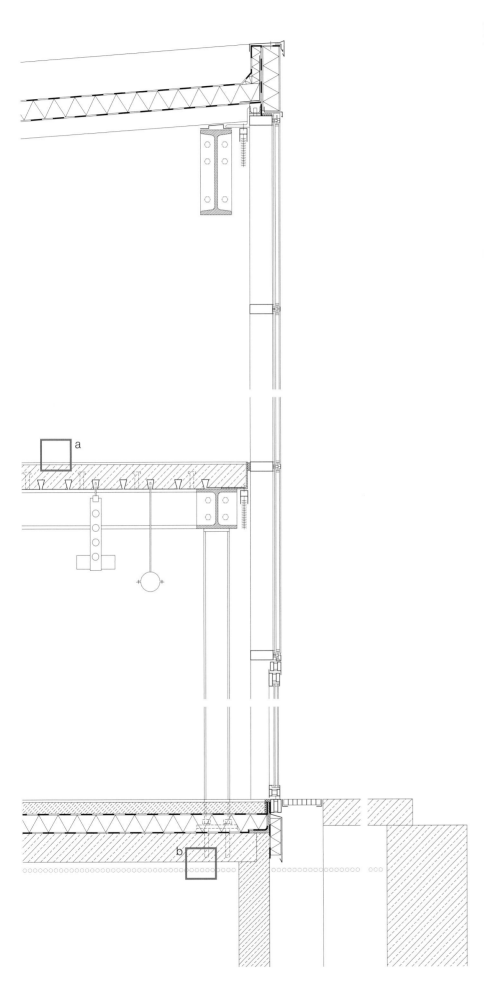

□ a
The mezzanine floor is constructed as a composite slab. In this example, a galvanised and coated profiled sheeting with dovetail slots on the underside is used in conjunction with a concrete topping. The edges are reinforced with sheet metal which at the same time serves as permanent formwork for the edges of the concrete topping. Composite columns and slabs with reinforcement in the concrete have a higher fire resistance than steel on its own and therefore do not need to be clad (see also page 16).

□ b
The columns to the mezzanine floor are mainly loaded in compression. At the top and bottom they are held in position which means that the column base requires only a simple connection. Such steel components, e.g. barriers, facade members, but also columns that need to be held in position only, are secured with drilled anchors, normally undercut anchors. However, if higher loads have to be accommodated, resin or bonded anchors can be used, but these entail more work during erection. After drilling a hole in the concrete, the hole is cleaned out and filled with a two-part resin mixture into which a threaded bar or an anchor is inserted as accurately as possible. After the resin has cured, the component can be bolted into place. Construction tolerances and subsequent changes to the layout can therefore be compensated for, taking into account the edge clearance distances and thicknesses of the components, and the erection work can continue without interruption.

Example A
Section through glass facade

□ a

In order that the glass appears as a large, uninterrupted, transparent surface, this facade is built as a curtain wall. Fixed glazing, opening lights, spandrel panels and sunshading can all be integrated into one building system to create a homogeneous building envelope. This system consists of a supporting framework of rectangular hollow sections positioned independently of the vertical loadbearing construction and fixed merely to the edge of the roof, edge of mezzanine floor slab and ground slab. If the panes of glass are glued to the supporting framework and the joints filled with silicone, then the construction is classed as a structural glazing facade (see page 27). However, in Germany such systems employing adhesive only are not permitted above a height of 8 m. Approved "all-glass facades" more than 8 m above ground level must include additional mechanical fixings, e.g. concealed bolts, as a back-up should the adhesive fail.

□ b

Glass, owing to its brittle nature, is susceptible to stress peaks caused by restraint, and therefore the supporting framework is connected to the loadbearing structure in such a way that movement due to differential deformations can be accommodated. Sliding connections (in this example at the eaves) or elongated holes which allow the fixings to move (in this example at the mezzanine floor) prevent the (permissible) deflections of the loadbearing structure from being transferred to the glass facade. By contrast, the fixing at the base of the facade does not permit any movement.

□ c

In order to be able to adjust the facade construction, the steel sections are fixed via bracket-type steel angles. Their elongated holes permit movement during erection, and this enables tolerances to be compensated for in three directions. The steel sections are fitted with plastic holders in order to create a thermal break between facade and supporting construction (see page 27). Interior fittings and furnishings are easily connected to the rectangular hollow sections. This is more difficult with open steel sections, which, on the other hand, do permit a differentiated design of the supporting framework.

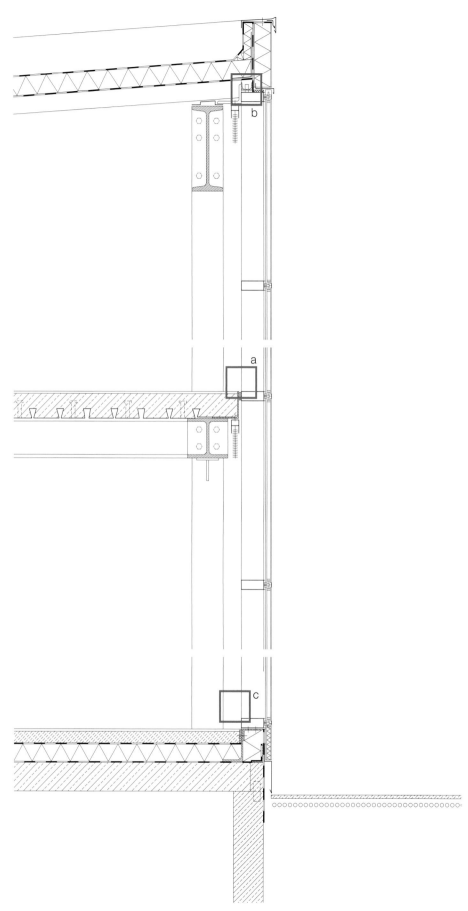

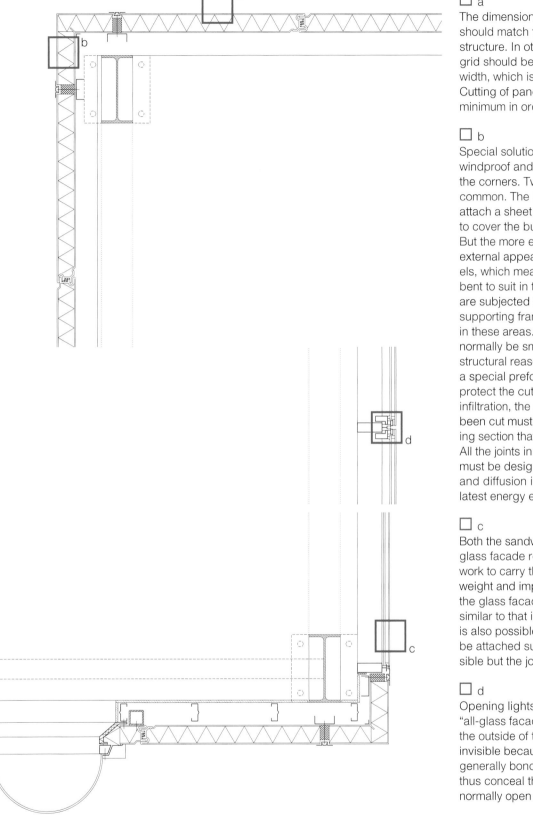

☐ a

The dimensions of the sandwich panels should match the grid of the loadbearing structure. In other words, the structural grid should be a multiple of the panel width, which is normally 0.90 to 1.10 m. Cutting of panels should be reduced to a minimum in order to keep costs down.

☐ b

Special solutions are required to create windproof and rainproof connections at the corners. Two variations have become common. The simplest method is to attach a sheet metal angle to the outside to cover the butt joint between the panels. But the more elegant solution for the external appearance is to use bent panels, which means the panels are cut and bent to suit in the works. As the corners are subjected to higher wind loads, the supporting framework must be reinforced in these areas. The corner panels must normally be smaller for geometrical and structural reasons, and waterproofed with a special preformed gasket. In order to protect the cut edges against moisture infiltration, the ends of panels that have been cut must be protected with a clamping section that is held at base and eaves. All the joints in the sandwich panel facade must be designed to prevent convection and diffusion in order to comply with latest energy efficiency regulations.

☐ c

Both the sandwich panel walls and the glass facade require a supporting framework to carry the loads due to wind, self-weight and impact. At the junction with the glass facade, a recessed joint feature similar to that in the sandwich panel walls is also possible. The glass facade must be attached such that movement is possible but the joints still remain windproof.

☐ d

Opening lights can be integrated into "all-glass facades". They are flush with the outside of the glass and are virtually invisible because the panes of glass are generally bonded over the frames and thus conceal them. The opening lights normally open outwards.

Example A
Composite floor, window strip

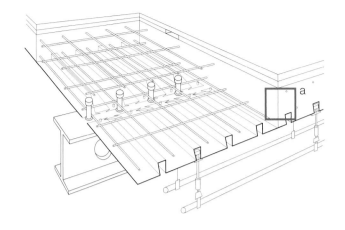

☐ a
Composite floors improve fire protection
and can be constructed using trapezoidal
profile or dovetail-slot sheeting. The sheet
metal serves as permanent formwork and
as the tension reinforcement in the floor
slab. At the same time, it creates a finished
soffit ready to accommodate hangers for
services. The sheet metal may need to be
supported during concreting operations,
depending on the span. Composite action
with the main beams is achieved by way
of shear studs welded to the top flanges.
Composite floors require building authority approval. Steel trapezoidal profile
sheeting is covered by DIN 18807.

☐ b
Lighting, ventilation and smoke/heat dissipation for the building are achieved by
way of windows and rooflights. The pro-
portion of customary window areas is not
usually sufficient, especially with large
building volumes.
The requirements are laid down in various
documents such as DIN 18232, the Industrial Buildings Directive and DIN 5034
"Daylight in interiors". Smoke-and-heat
vents are necessary to ensure that life-
threatening fumes can escape in the
event of a fire. The vents are opened
automatically by means of electric or
pneumatic drives during a fire.
The rooflights (see page 17) can also be
opened manually in normal situations.
To ensure circulation of the air, inlets
must be provided, e.g. in the facades.

☐ c
Although in this project the rooflights
ensure adequate lighting and ventilation,
horizontal and vertical sections through
industrial glazing are drawn here as an
example. Single glazing options provide
adequate lighting for unheated shed
areas. Instead of elaborate window elements, translucent profiled glass can be
used – channel-shaped cast glass sections manufactured in a mechanical rolling method. Standard opening lights can
be incorporated to permit a view through
to the outside, as recommended by the
Places of Work Directive for every work-
place, and to provide ventilation.
The building performance disadvantage
of the limited thermal insulation can be
ignored in this situation.

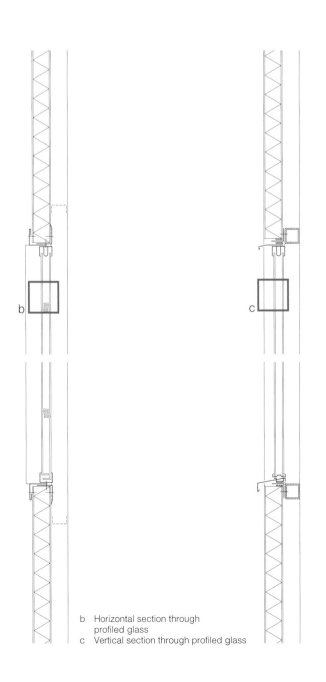

b   Horizontal section through
    profiled glass
c   Vertical section through profiled glass

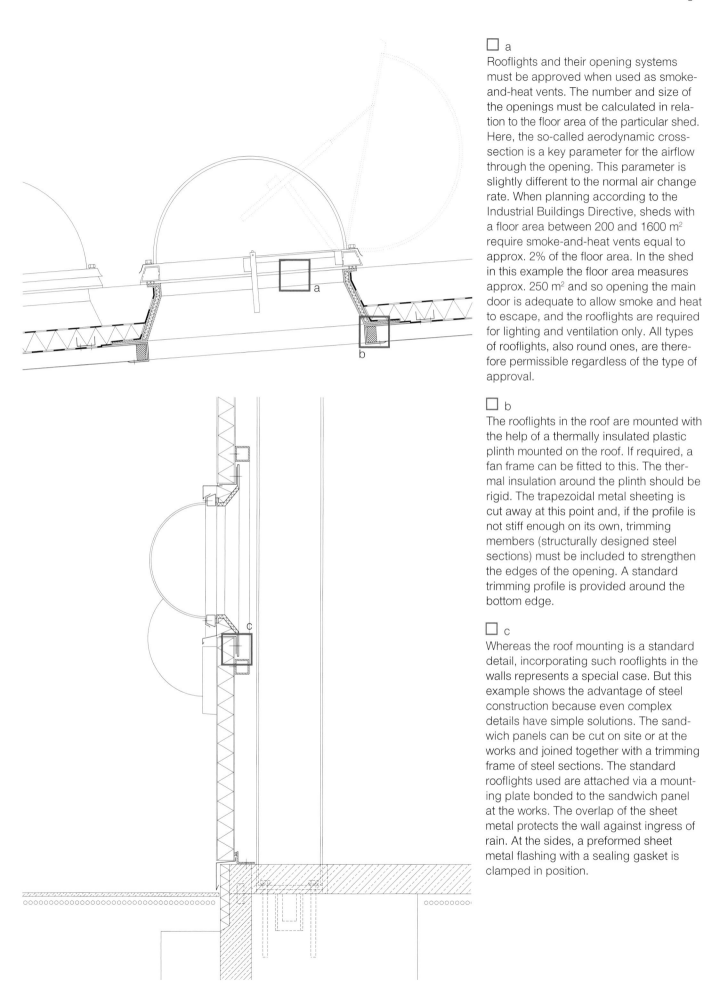

☐ a
Rooflights and their opening systems must be approved when used as smoke-and-heat vents. The number and size of the openings must be calculated in relation to the floor area of the particular shed. Here, the so-called aerodynamic cross-section is a key parameter for the airflow through the opening. This parameter is slightly different to the normal air change rate. When planning according to the Industrial Buildings Directive, sheds with a floor area between 200 and 1600 m² require smoke-and-heat vents equal to approx. 2% of the floor area. In the shed in this example the floor area measures approx. 250 m² and so opening the main door is adequate to allow smoke and heat to escape, and the rooflights are required for lighting and ventilation only. All types of rooflights, also round ones, are therefore permissible regardless of the type of approval.

☐ b
The rooflights in the roof are mounted with the help of a thermally insulated plastic plinth mounted on the roof. If required, a fan frame can be fitted to this. The thermal insulation around the plinth should be rigid. The trapezoidal metal sheeting is cut away at this point and, if the profile is not stiff enough on its own, trimming members (structurally designed steel sections) must be included to strengthen the edges of the opening. A standard trimming profile is provided around the bottom edge.

☐ c
Whereas the roof mounting is a standard detail, incorporating such rooflights in the walls represents a special case. But this example shows the advantage of steel construction because even complex details have simple solutions. The sandwich panels can be cut on site or at the works and joined together with a trimming frame of steel sections. The standard rooflights used are attached via a mounting plate bonded to the sandwich panel at the works. The overlap of the sheet metal protects the wall against ingress of rain. At the sides, a preformed sheet metal flashing with a sealing gasket is clamped in position.

Example A
Overhead door

☐ a
One essential component of every industrial shed is a large, easily usable opening which allows trouble-free delivery and collection of goods and materials.
The wind loads, the weight of the door and its movement call for an elaborate secondary structure which must be integrated into the planning at an early stage in order to achieve a coherent design. As a rule, we distinguish between four types of door:
• folding
• horizontal or vertical sliding
• overhead
• roller shutter

Criteria for selecting doors are size of opening, speed of operation, space requirements and the opening mechanism. In simple single-storey sheds, an overhead door is often used because it has proved economic and quick to open/close for small and medium sizes (up to 7 m high x 8 m wide).
Sliding or folding doors are used for larger openings. In terms of space requirement when open, the roller shutter door, with its individual slats rolled up behind the lintel over the opening, is unbeatable. The interlinked single- or double-wall slats are fitted with end caps to prevent lateral displacement. Roller shutters are mainly used for narrow and high openings, but widths up to 25 m are also possible.

☐ b
Overhead doors consist of a few transverse elements connected together with hinges, and can be made from thermally insulated sandwich panels. The interlinked elements slide – operated electrically or manually – in rails on both sides and are parked beneath the roof of the shed. Torsion springs – possibly tension springs in the case of smaller doors – adjacent to the lintel compensate for the weight. The space requirement at the sides is similar to that for a roller shutter door, but the guiding depth is somewhat greater. Wicket-gates can be formed within the main door.

☐ c
In order to avoid air circulation in the trapezoidal profile sheeting at the junction with the facade, profile filler pieces can be inserted. These are made from rigid foam profiles. Sheet metal to match the profile is screwed on to protect the foam and prevent the ingress of insects.

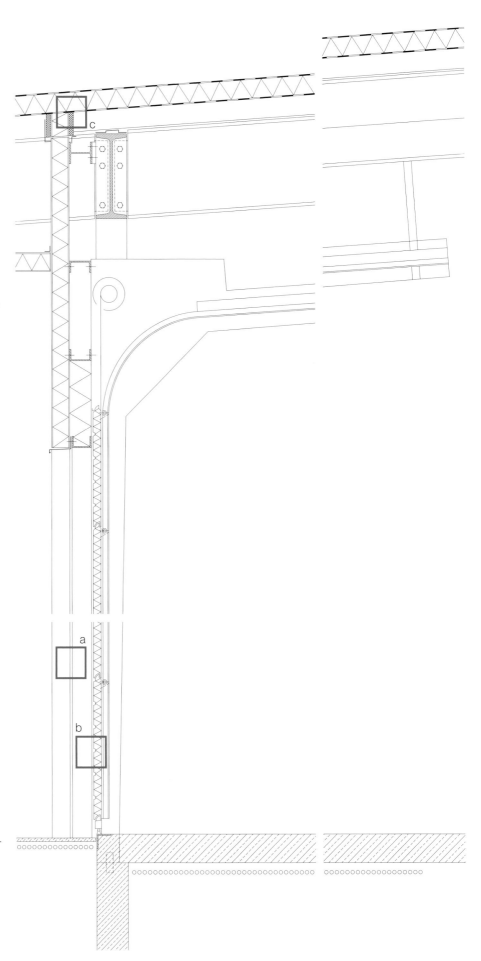

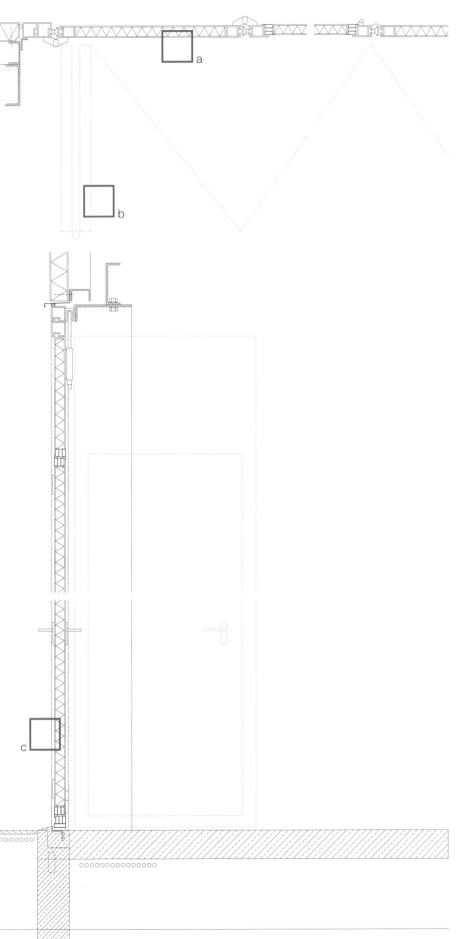

□ a
Folding doors are easy to build into the structure thanks to their peripheral frame. They are available with sandwich panels or glazing and must always be fitted with cushioning end buffers to prevent injuries. The roller guides permit manual operation of even large, multi-leaf doors.
In the case of very large openings, e.g. aircraft hangars, sliding doors are often used which are normally supported on rollers at the bottom with an additional guide track at the top in order to be able to handle the enormous self-weight of the leaves and so that no leaf remains standing in the opening. Sliding doors can be divided into bottom-track, top-track and cantilevering versions depending on how the weight of the door is supported.

□ b
Steel folding doors are multi-leaf variants with relieving rollers whose individual elements concertina to left or right, with the folded door positioned inside or outside. The type of operation must be taken into account to ensure that there is enough space for the folded door leaves when the door is open. The space requirement can be quite considerable for wide doors and it should be remembered that 90° folding will reduce the clear width of the opening. Folding through 180° and parking in front of the facade is also possible, but complicated.

□ c
In the event of fire or for the passage of persons, opening such large doors takes too long and involves too much effort. Therefore, folding, sliding and overhead doors can be fitted with wicket-gates. These single-leaf, side-hung doors are integrated into the main door and can be designed with or without a threshold. An electrical contact prevents the main door being opened if a wicket-gate is left open. Folding doors can have one leaf designed to open separately instead of a wicket-gate. Such leaves do not have a threshold and if they are high can be divided horizontally at a convenient height. This option achieves a larger clear opening than a wicket-gate and hardly intrudes on the overall design of the door.

A folding door has been used for this example because it can reflect the vertical lines of the sandwich panels and also gives the facade an uninterrupted, flush appearance.

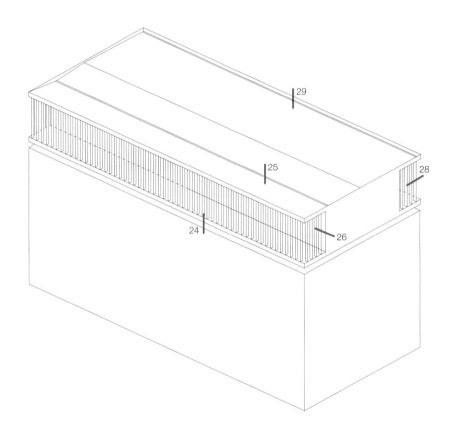

Overview of details
scale 1:20

24   Section through loggia
25   Section through glass facade
26   Horizontal section through loggia
27   Glazing systems
28   Horizontal section through steel pan wall
29   Vertical section through steel pan wall

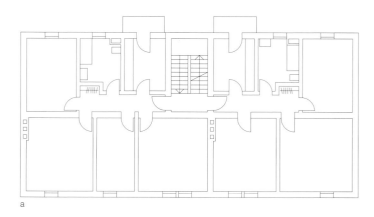

a

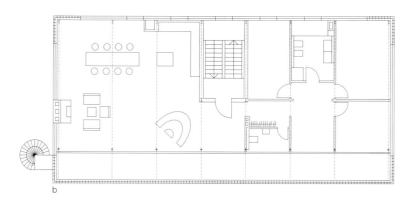

b

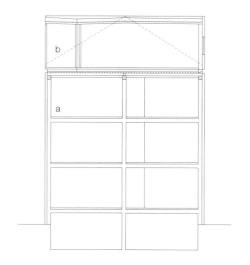

b

a

Other typical applications for steel structures are extensions or rooftop structures as part of refurbishment and conversion projects involving existing buildings. Owing to the high degree of prefabrication, its readiness to redistribute loads and its low self-weight, steel is ideal for rooftop structures. In this example the aim is not to achieve a dramatic redesign or marked increase in height, but rather to achieve a simple and appropriate solution for a fictitious building dating from the 1950s or 1960s which, as part of urban upgrading, for example, is to be given an additional storey.

Our fictitious existing building has three storeys and a pitched roof, and carries the loads via the external and central masonry walls. Access to the apartments is via a central staircase on the north side. The additional storey covers the entire plan area of the building and access is via the existing staircase. The regulations do not require a lift in buildings of only four storeys, although the inclusion of a lift is to be recommended when designing for elderly or disabled occupants.

The existing pitched roof, a straightforward timber structure, is removed and a new steel construction erected on the existing loadbearing walls. The floor slab over the existing building is built as a composite floor in order to satisfy the fire protection and sound insulation requirements, but the roof over the new storey can be a simpler and lighter all-steel construction because there are no habitable rooms above. The facade to the new storey consists of full-height sliding windows and sheet steel pans with air cavity plus a lining of plasterboard on the inside and horizontal sheet metal panels on the outside. One spacious penthouse-type apartment with a rooftop terrace is intended.

As the actual facade is set back to create the terrace, this reduces the floor area of the apartment itself and in some regions of Germany this is then no longer counted as a storey proper, meaning that certain building regulations are eased. In the example given here, the set-back facade is used to create a loggia, which has vertical sunshading elements that enhance the consistent and hence restrained design of the additional storey.

Scale 1:250
a   Existing building
b   Additional storey

The exploded isometric view shows the relationship between supports, loadbearing construction and bracing using an additional storey as an example. The load-distributing layer, the "foundation" of the extension, is in this example in the form of a concrete capping beam cast on top of the existing masonry, which creates a consistent base for the new steel structure.

The primary structure consists of rolled steel sections connected to form propped cantilever frames, each "prop" of which is a pinned-end column made from four angle sections. Every frame is supported on a continuous I-beam (HEA section) which spans across the central wall from one external wall to the other. The additional support on the central wall helps to reduce the size of the steel section and exploit evenly the load-carrying reserves of the existing building. Rebuilding the suspended floor is generally advisable because the topmost floors of older buildings are not usually designed for heavier loads, and in some cases the topmost floor, between top storey and attic, is not even a concrete slab. The spacing of the frames depends on the maximum span of the trapezoidal profile sheeting being used, which in this example serves as permanent formwork and secondary structure. In order to avoid all temporary propping during concreting, or at least to reduce this to one temporary prop per bay, the spacing of the frames should not be too large. The maximum permissible span of the trapezoidal profile sheeting depends on the depth of the profile, the thickness of the sheet metal and whether the profile is stiffened by additional ribs. Such sheeting can span up to 5 m, but 2 to 3 m is advisable. Despite the extra work required, the main beams and the metal sheeting serving as the secondary beams are erected in one plane in order to minimise the height of the additional storey.
The bracing to the structural steelwork in the longitudinal direction is in the form of X-bracing at roof level, which is mounted directly over the trapezoidal profile sheeting and transfers the loads to the walls of the staircase. The frames themselves brace the new storey in the transverse direction.

The roof to the loggia is supported on cantilever beams and is hence part of the actual frame construction. However, there is a thermal break separating these from the loadbearing structure in the heated part of the building which takes the form of a thermally insulated structural element.

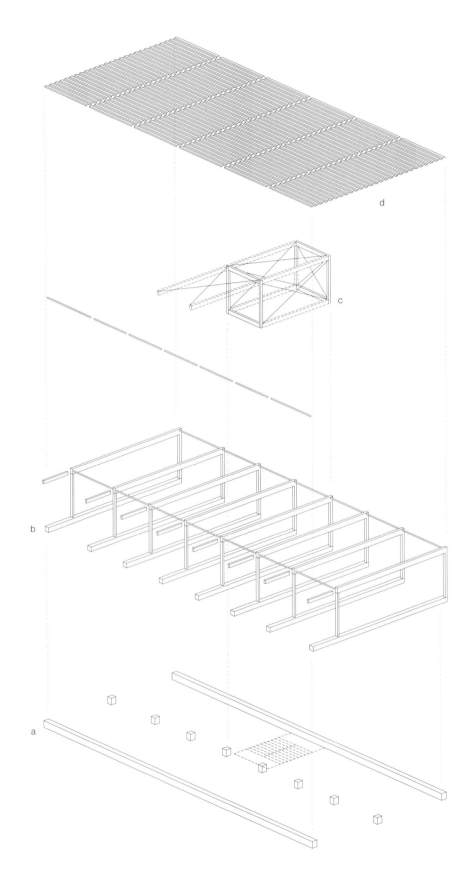

a   Load-distributing capping beam plus individual supports
b   Primary loadbearing structure: propped cantilever frames with pinned-end columns
c   Stiffening core with struts
d   Secondary loadbearing structure: trapezoidal profile sheeting

The enclosing envelope gives the new storey its external appearance. It is designed as a rational, smooth steel facade which emphasizes the character of the material. The special characteristic of factory-made metal facades is their modular construction and accurate finishing. The "box" is recognisable as a new structure placed on top of the refurbished building. In order to achieve the image of an enclosing envelope, the sunshading in this example is formed by vertical louvres integrated flush with the facade, and on the north side by sliding shutters in front of the windows.

The enclosing envelope to a frame structure is a non-loadbearing external wall which functions exclusively as an enclosing element providing protection from the weather. We distinguish between the following types of non-loadbearing envelope:

- Single-leaf, uninsulated walls, e.g. corrugated or trapezoidal profile sheeting of different thicknesses and with different profiles, which are mounted directly on the supporting construction.
- Single-leaf, insulated walls consisting of a weatherproof skin, thermal insulation and internal lining, but no air cavity. One example of such a multi-layer, single-leaf construction is the sandwich panel, which consists of profiled sheet steel facings and a core of thermal insulation bonded rigidly together.
- Double-leaf, insulated walls. Different wall constructions are possible, but the outer leaf, the weatherproof skin, is always separated from the other layers by an air cavity. The internal leaf can consist of profiled metal sheeting with any kind of shaping, or solid materials (non-loadbearing masonry, autoclaved aerated concrete) to which the thermal insulation and the external leaf of profiled metal sheeting or sheet metal pans are attached.

The construction of the walls depends on functional requirements regarding thermal, sound and fire performance.
In the example shown here, steel pans with thermal insulation behind sheet metal panels, with an air cavity between the two, have been used.

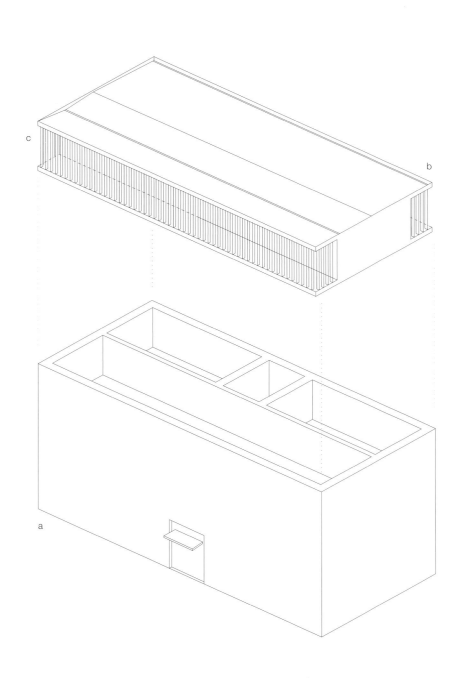

a   Existing building
b   Additional storey
c   Sunshading

Example B
Section through loggia

□ a

A concrete capping beam has been cast
onto the existing external wall of clay
bricks in order to achieve a consistent,
firm support, to compensate for the tolerances after demolition work, and to stabilise the masonry walls. The wide I-beams
(HEA sections), economic rolled sections
with a broad cross-section, are then
placed directly on the concrete, with
packing pieces or shims as required to
achieve the right level, and secured with
drilled anchors.

□ b

The trapezoidal profile sheeting is laid
directly on the top flange of the I-beam
and provided with a trimming angle along
the edge which links the steel beams
together and secures them against lateral
buckling. The trapezoidal profile sheeting
serves as permanent formwork (to DIN
18867-3). Reinforcement is placed in the
ribs of the concrete topping and so the
floor acts as a ribbed slab. Adequate
concrete cover to the reinforcement
ensures good fire resistance qualities.
This concrete floor functions as a stiffening diaphragm and achieves a composite
action with the steel beams through the
shear studs welded to the top flanges of
the beams (see page 16). In a composite
floor, the concrete carries the compressive loads very efficiently and ensures
economic, long-lasting fire protection.
The fire resistance of the trapezoidal profile sheeting can be enhanced – up to
class F90 – if the suspended ceiling used
in this example is omitted. To do this, the
spaces between the ribs can be filled
with concrete, or the steel can be given
a coat of intumescent paint (approved up
to F90, see page 84). It is also possible
to spray on a cement-based plaster reinforced with synthetic fibres.

□ c

In order to differentiate between old and
new, a recessed joint is used to highlight
the transition. A sheet metal flashing,
clipped and riveted to the underlying construction, closes off the thermal insulation
composite system added to the existing
building during the course of the refurbishment work and thus forms the transition to
the new storey.

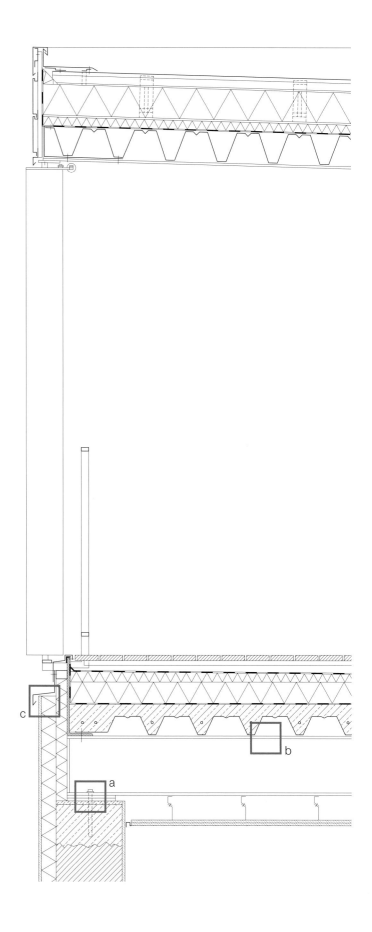

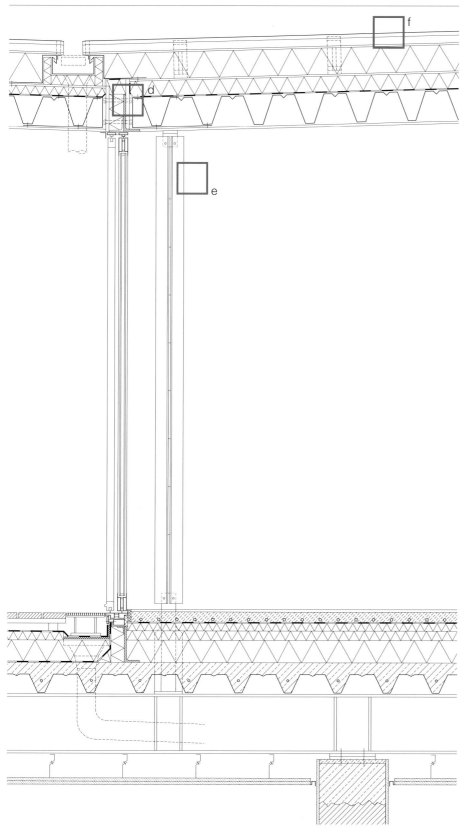

☐ d
The cantilever beams of the loggia canopy, which protects against rain and sunshine, and the primary loadbearing frames are connected via a structural thermal insulation element. This standard element designed to create a thermal break between steel sections minimises the heat transmission and hence prevents the formation of condensation. The – in structural terms – continuous steel beam is split into two parts joined together with end plates positioned either side of rigid insulation to which threaded bars are attached, the size of which depends on the respective forces and moments to be transferred across this joint.
This enables the appearance of the exposed steel beams and trapezoidal profile sheeting soffit to be continued through to the loggia and avoids the need to enclose the canopy in thermal insulation – an expensive undertaking. The insulation shown here is provided merely as anti-drumming protection and to avoid a step in the level of the roof finishes.

☐ e
The connection to the pinned-end column is a hinge in structural terms, which means that only axial forces, e.g. from the roof loads, can be transmitted across the joint, but no bending moments. In order to feature this structural connection architecturally as well, the column is separated visually from the soffit and the floor, and the forces are transferred via narrow plates in the middle of the four angles forming the cruciform section.

☐ f
The roof of loadbearing trapezoidal profile sheeting is designed as a warm deck and is finished with a system of industrially prefabricated profiled panels. These panels, which can be laid on roofs with a pitch as shallow as 1.5°, are joined on site by bending up the edges with a machine to form an interlocking, rainproof joint. The panels are then fixed by means of special clips fitted into the turned-up edges which are clipped onto a rail placed on the lower, rigid layer of insulation. As these rails are fixed to the loadbearing trapezoidal profile sheeting at individual points only, the wind pressure and suction forces are transferred to the loadbearing construction virtually without creating any thermal bridges. The special clips/turned-up edges arrangement permits unhindered expansion of the profiled panels, even long panels, in conjunction with thermal insulation up to 300 mm thick.

Example B
Horizontal section through loggia

☐ a
The pinned-end columns behind the glass facade are made up of four angle sections, which gives them a highly sculpted look. Narrow plates in the middle of the cruciform section are used to join the angles together. The hinged connections at top and bottom are also achieved by means of narrow plates or T-pieces.

☐ b
A grating in front of the glass facade ensures that the water run-off layer is 150 mm lower, as required by the DIN standard. This also acts as a drainage channel for the rooftop terrace when the fall is such that the terrace drains towards this. Such channels and their associated downpipes, which are essentially within the building, require special care during construction to avoid all leaks. Therefore, all joints must be watertight (soldered, welded, glued). The bituminous felt or other waterproofing material must be fixed to a firm substrate, e.g. a panel or sheet metal attached to the base of the facade. If the waterproofing is merely bonded to the insulation at this point, it could be damaged by foot traffic (see page 25 also).

☐ c
The sunshade consists of movable, vertical aluminium louvres coupled together to form groups. Electric motors are used to adjust the angle of each group of louvres.

☐ d
The building authorities require a safety barrier behind the sunshade. This is fixed to the trimming angle along the outer edge of the terrace because this is the best place for waterproofing it (see also page 24). The floor finish to the terrace consists of a timber grid which allows rain and snow to drain through and enables a flush transition between inside and outside.

☐ e
On-site connections in structural steelwork should be bolted whenever possible in order to avoid on-site welding damaging the corrosion protection of prefabricated elements. The easier it is to reach the bolted connections, the more economic is the construction. The bolts should also remain readily accessible for maintenance purposes.

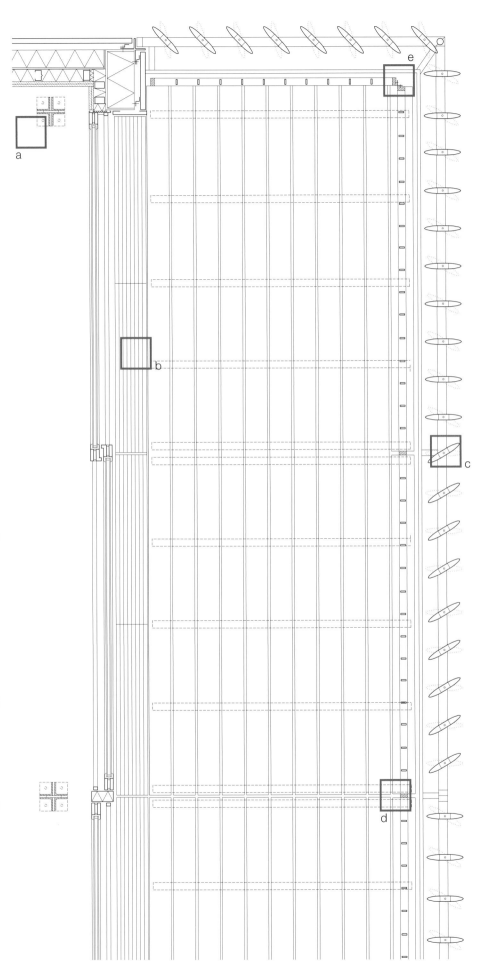

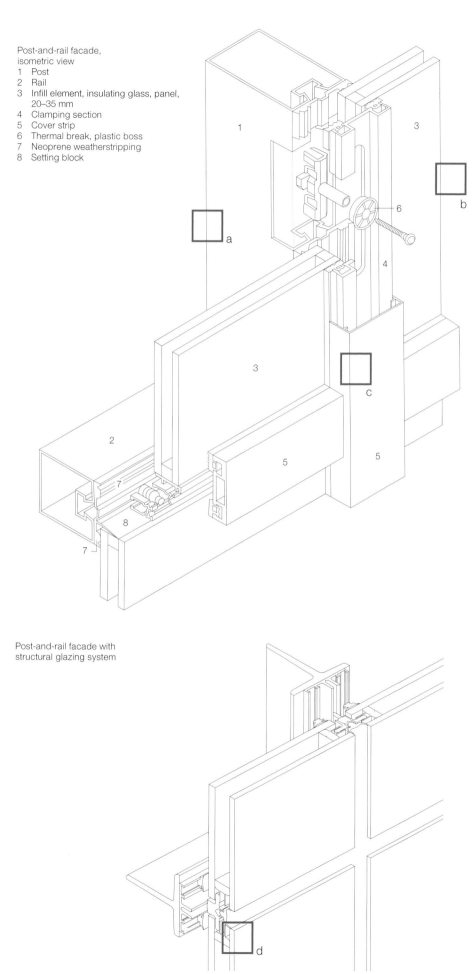

Post-and-rail facade,
isometric view
1   Post
2   Rail
3   Infill element, insulating glass, panel,
    20–35 mm
4   Clamping section
5   Cover strip
6   Thermal break, plastic boss
7   Neoprene weatherstripping
8   Setting block

Post-and-rail facade with
structural glazing system

☐ a
Transparent suspended facades (curtain
walls) in structural steelwork are normally
designed as post-and-rail assemblies.
The vertical posts and the horizontal rails
made from steel sections form the supporting framework, the dimensions of
which are calculated to suit the structural
requirements. Owing to their physical
properties, steel sections can be designed
as very slender, even for longer spans.
Either the post or the rail can assume the
primary loadbearing function. Neoprene
gaskets (see no. 4 and 7) are required to
seal the joint between glass and steel and
to waterproof the rebate for the glass, and
these are pressed into pre-cut slots in the
steel members.

☐ b
The glazing is normally in the form of
insulating glass units whose configuration
and coatings are designed to satisfy various functions such as thermal performance, fire protection or solar-control.

☐ c
The outer clamping strip is screwed to the
supporting construction to generate a
predefined clamping pressure. Separating the steel frame by means of plastic
strips achieves a thermal break in the
facade. The cover strips are available in
various shapes and materials. The horizontal and vertical weatherstripping over-
laps at the intersections. Brackets, which
pass through the cover strips, can be
fixed to the steel sections for attaching
external sunshades.

☐ d
If a flush external appearance is required
for the glass facade, then a structural
glazing system must be employed. In this
case the panes of glass are not held in
place by clamping strips, but instead by
clips which fit into the rebate at the edge
of the pane. The outer pane of insulating
glass is essentially held by the adhesive
of the hermetic edge seal, but also has
individual mechanical fixings that differ
depending on the system (which must be
approved by the building authority). The
mechanical fixings are covered by the
silicone subsequently injected into the
joint (see page 14).

Example B
Horizontal section through steel pan wall

□ a

In order to emphasize the contrast between the closed and open walls, the glazed corner should be as transparent as possible. The panes of glass at the corner are held on three sides only; the fourth side has a stepped joint, which permits a frameless corner detail. To prevent the hermetic edge seal of insulating glass being exposed to damaging ultraviolet radiation, an enamel finish to the edge seal is recommended. The open joint is then sealed with silicone.

□ b

Steel pans form the main body of the wall. Pans are channel-shaped sheet metal elements, approx. 1 mm thick and up to 21 m long, which are attached to the primary structure and filled with thermal insulating material. The approx. 500–600 mm wide steel pans span horizontally from column to column and, provided the span is not too great, require no further supports. The profile of the pans is such that they are stabilised against buckling and have turned-up edges for fixing the outer leaf, which is connected directly to the steel pans by means of self-tapping screws, self-drilling screws or rivets. To improve the thermal performance, the outer leaf, the pan and in this case the steel framework, too, are separated thermally by a foam strip and the joints between the pans are closed off windtight by sealing strips. In the example shown here, sheet metal panels are used for the outer leaf (fitted clear of the pans to create an air cavity) instead of the more usual trapezoidal profile sheeting. Another layer of insulation with a lining of plasterboard has also been fitted in this example. A supporting framework of rectangular hollow sections is therefore required for fixing the steel pans in this example.

Walls consisting of steel pans are assigned to building materials class A2, which eases the fire protection requirements. Perforated steel pans can help to improve the acoustic performance.

□ c

One possible solution for the corner of a wall of steel pans: the pans are buttjointed, and the joint between the outer leaf of sheet metal panels is closed off with a standard sheet metal corner profile.

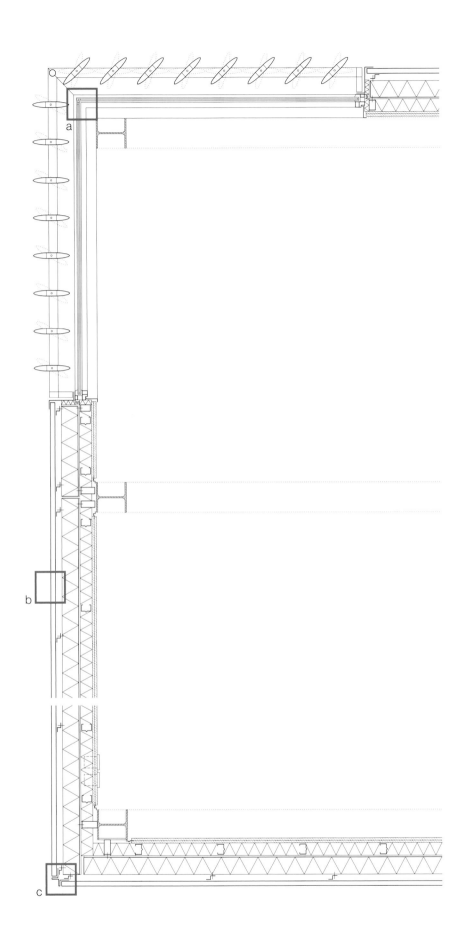

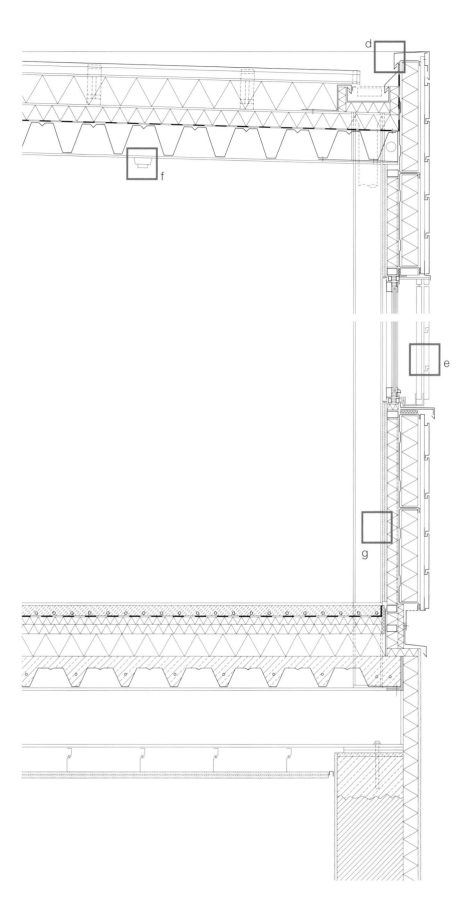

☐ d

The detail at the top of the wall must be planned very carefully. The trimming angle and the fixing angle for the parapet must overlap. An internal gutter guarantees good drainage. The size of the gutter cross-section must be in accordance with DIN 18460 in order to prevent seepage below the waterproofing and thermal insulation.

☐ e

The panels of the outer leaf are perforated at the windows so that they can be used as sliding shutters and thus achieve a flush sunshading detail.

☐ f

Smoke detectors have been compulsory for residential buildings since 2005 in most of Germany's federal states. They are efficient warning systems and must be installed in bedrooms, hallways and corridors.
As this is a building with only a few storeys, there is only one additional storey and there are no further habitable rooms above the new construction, the steel members in this example can be left exposed and do not require any further fire protection measures.

☐ g

An installation layer has been included on the inside of the wall construction for accommodating electric sockets or other cable/pipes as required. This layer is finished with two sheets of plasterboard ready to receive the decorative finishes.

Designing the loadbearing structure

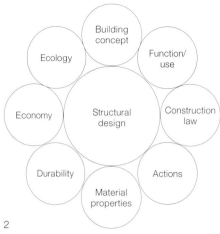

1 Centred space frame
   Velodrome, Berlin, 1996,
   Dominique Perrault
2 Boundary conditions for structural design

The evolution of a loadbearing structure

The design of a loadbearing structure is a game involving forces and the forms of the paths these forces take in travelling from their place of action to their goals, the supports. The design of the loadbearing structure is, in principle, different to its structural analysis, in which the prime consideration is to determine the proper and comprehensible stability of a loadbearing structure that has already been planned. The design of the loadbearing structure and the development of constructional solutions are derived from the architectural concept and must take account of numerous boundary conditions.

The inseparable link between structural form and architectural design calls for a close and early collaboration between architect and engineer because this is the only way that synergies resulting from functionality and design can be integrated into the concept. This results in almost infinite design options, depending on the economic considerations.

The function of the loadbearing structure is to carry loads and transfer these to points designated or useful as supports. We divide the loads into dead and imposed loads which depend on the use of the structure and the climatic conditions. When devising a loadbearing structure, the system of forces describes the constructional task of transferring the forces from their points of application to the supports. The system of forces is defined by the magnitudes, distributions, directions and points of application of the loads plus the positions of the supports. The loadbearing system, often also called the structural system, can be developed from the system of forces. The loadbearing system is defined by the system dimensions (e.g. spacing of columns), the

form (external geometry), the support conditions (e.g. non-sway, sway, fixed) and the loading. It is the loadbearing system that forms the basis for the structural analysis.

Besides the constructional boundary conditions, which are formulated in the system of forces, numerous other influences have to be considered, including economic aspects, durability and erection sequence, provided the design team is applying an integrated approach to the design.

Just like the architectural design initially requires a concept developed from urban, sociological and functional requirements, the structural design requires a concept for carrying the loads. This latter concept has to take into account the constructional boundary conditions, the design approaches and the expectations regarding the durability and economics of a particular construction.

Owing to its easy shaping and the possibilities for assembling single components and adapting them to the loadings in the structure as a whole, steel is a building material that presents good conditions for optimising loadbearing structures with regard to the architectural and functional requirements. The number one form of construction for steel buildings is the frame, which in contrast to concrete and masonry structures is characterised by linear loadbearing members and the strict separation between loadbearing and enclosing (infill) components.

Optimising the structure with regard to the paths of the forces almost always leads to good "legibility" of the structural logic. In doing so, the designer has to decide whether to expose the structural members or conceal them, in which case they become merely functional elements. The two examples demonstrate the

advantages of structural steelwork for buildings (pages 8–19 and 20–29).

The advantages of structural steelwork for additional storeys or conversions:
- "Dry" building site and short construction time thanks to prefabrication of the primary structure.
- Low self-weight of the construction, which therefore makes allowance for the limited load-carrying capacity of the existing building.
- Appropriate prefabrication leads to easy erection.
- Low structural depths through selecting sections suitable for the loads and thanks to the efficiency of steel.
- Frame construction results in generous design options for plan layout and building envelope.
- Integration of unclad primary structural elements into the interior design through corresponding details.

The advantages of structural steelwork for single-storey sheds:
- Construction of long spans with a delicate structure by adapting the section geometries to the internal force distributions.
- Integration of the building services taking into account the paths of the forces in the primary building components.
- Short erection times and simple building site facilities thanks to the high degree of prefabrication.
- By separating structure and envelope, frame construction offers the opportunity for large door openings.

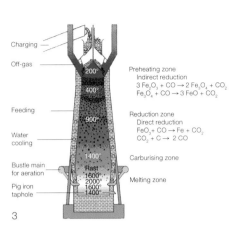

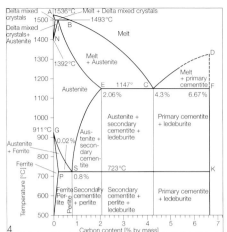

3 The blast-furnace process
Source: *Didaktik der Chemie*, 08/1997,
University of Bayreuth
4 Iron-carbon phase diagram
States of steel and iron in relation to temperature
and carbon content
Source: Polytechnic of Mechanical Engineering,
www.maschinenbau-fh.de

Steel production

Steel, certainly the most important metal for the construction industry, is a malleable iron with a carbon content of max. 2%. It can therefore be called an alloy of iron and carbon which contains further accompanying and alloying elements. Structural steels generally have a carbon content < 0.25%. The accompanying elements include phosphorus, sulphur and nitrogen. The most important alloying elements are chromium, manganese, aluminium, molybdenum and nickel.

The basic material for producing steel is pig iron obtained from a blast-furnace. A blast-furnace is a huge vessel up to 100 m high which is lined with firebricks and clad in a steel jacket. It is fed from above with a mixture of iron ore (iron oxide), limestone (= burden) and coke. Iron is the fourth commonest chemical element in the Earth's crust. In its natural form it exists as a base metal in an oxidised state. Rocks with an iron content exceeding 20% are suitable for smelting and are collectively known as iron ore. Crushing and screening break down the ore and coke raw materials into equal-sized pieces.
In order to integrate the dust components and improve the flow of gases through the charging stock in the blast-furnace shaft, the ore is baked (sintered) with coke and limestone, or pelletised as a granulate.
The blast-furnace process reduces the oxygen bonded in the iron ore. The coke reacts with the hot air introduced via the bustle main to form carbon monoxide, which in turn reduces the iron ore to pig iron in a redox reaction and is itself further oxidised to form carbon dioxide.
The two carbon oxide forms escape through the throat, the topmost part of the blast-furnace, and are fed to the air preheaters. Here, the combustible carbon

monoxide is ignited and used to heat up the air, which is fed back into the blast-furnace via the bustle main.

Modern blast-furnaces can produce more than 10 000 tonnes of pig iron every day. Their average service life – in which the blast-furnace process runs unceasingly – is 10 years.

The pig iron obtained in this way contains 3.5–4.5% carbon as well as other disruptive accompanying elements which make it brittle and cause it to soften immediately upon being heated. In order to convert the pig iron into steel, the carbon content must be lowered and the accompanying elements, principally sulphur, reduced or removed. This is essentially done by blowing oxygen or air into the molten pig iron and by deoxidising it through the addition of limestone slag.
The many different methods for producing the crude steel are mainly distinguished by the way in which the oxygen is fed and the heat applied. The best-known methods are the basic Bessemer process with its converter and oxygen lances, the open-hearth furnace with the addition of steel scrap, and the electric-arc furnace.
In the melt, the carbon and iron atoms arrange themselves into various crystal lattice structures depending on the temperature and the carbon content. The iron-carbon phase diagram in fig. 4 defines the various transition zones for iron and steel.

The speed with which the crude steel is cooled determines the form of the crystals in the final product. The chief structural forms for the ranges of applications for structural steels are the fine-grained, face-centred austenitic steels (α-iron) and the body-centred ferritic steels (γ-iron) (see fig. 4). Different conditions regarding the granularity, embrittlement and ductility

owing to the temperature treatment of the crude steel are designated untreated, normalised or tempered.

In order to avoid bubble-like inclusions of oxygen or carbon residue, so-called segregation, when casting the steels, aluminium, silicon or manganese is added to the melt to "kill" it. Steels killed in this way are less sensitive to ageing and better for welding. Depending on the type of casting, we distinguish between unkilled (U), killed (R) and fully killed (RR) steels.

No other material is used for so many diverse applications in building as steel. Starting with supports for the excavations, continuing through reinforcing steel and anchors in the foundations, primary structural elements such as columns and beams, right up to facades and cladding and sheet metal components for the interior fittings, steel is employed in all phases of the erection of a structure.

Especially important for the building industry are the general mild and structural steels according to the definitions of DIN EN 10025, steels for reinforcing bars and welded meshes to DIN 488 (important for reinforced concrete construction), plus stainless steels, tempered steels for screws and bolts, and high-strength steels.
The main difference between stainless steel and everyday mild steel is the alloying with further chemical elements such as chromium, molybdenum and nickel. It should be remembered that stainless steels resist corrosion only in certain ambient conditions; only with a chromium content of about 17% is a higher corrosion resistance possible.
The use and application of the steels must be checked against the applicable building authority approvals for the respective type of application with respect

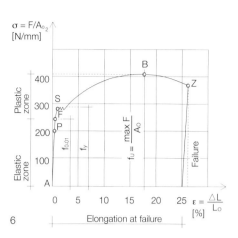

5 Breaking lengths [km] of various materials, defined as the ratio of the load-carrying capacity
   [N/mm²] to the load due to self-weight [N]
6 Stress-strain diagram for grade S235 steel
   σ = stress
   F = force
   A_o = original cross-sectional area
   ε = strain
   $\triangle L$ = change in length
   L_o = original length

Breaking length [km]

Grade S235 steel	5.2 km
Grade S355 steel	7.1 km
Grade C20/25 concrete	1.0 km[1]
Softwood	3.8 km
Titanium	17.8 km[2]
Carbon fibres	130.0 km
Cobweb fibres	70.0 km

[1] Related to the compressive strength
[2] Depends on type of alloy

Mechanical properties

The breaking length, a criterion frequently used to evaluate the efficiency of a building material, is the length at which a material fails in tension caused purely by the self-weight of the material itself. Comparing the breaking length of steel with those of other building materials reveals steel's enhanced efficiency compared to other traditional building materials like concrete and timber. However, it also demonstrates that further mechanical parameters are important for assessing the efficiency and usability of a building material. For example, the designer should check whether exploiting the load-carrying capacity results in deformations that are unacceptable for the type of construction selected and the type of use.

Structural steel is especially characterised by its high material stiffness, which in conjunction with its linear elastic behaviour up to the yield point is equal for both compressive and tensile loads. It is precisely this property that renders possible the wide use of steel and the exact calculation of deformations in the loadbearing structure.

When designing structural steelwork components, it is also possible to make use of the distinctive plastic behaviour of steel. This behaviour guarantees a high degree of safety because failure of a component does not take place suddenly as with a brittle material, but instead signals impending problems through significant deformations and a strain of up to 26%! At the same time, the plastic material behaviour enables a redistribution of loads from highly stressed to less highly stressed zones.

Besides the manifold adaptability of steel with regard to function and appearance, and the options for optimising the cross-section, it is in the first place the mechanical properties that are important when designing a loadbearing structure. The design, construction and monitoring of structural steelwork is essentially carried out on the basis of the series of structural steelwork standards DIN 18800 parts 1 to 7.

The stress-strain diagram shown in fig. 6 for steel grade S235 plus other material parameters are used below to describe the mechanical properties.
From fig. 6 it can be seen that steel behaves elastically in the range A to P and the strain is exactly proportional to the applied load. As point P is difficult to define owing to the gradual transition to the curve, the so-called elastic limit is specified for practical purposes, which has the defined, measurable property that the permanent plastic strain is just 0.01% (point F). Significant yielding of the material begins at point S (the yield point for a tensile test, the compressive yield point in a compression test), and the strain increases without an increase in the load. The strain from this point onwards is permanent and the material does not return to its original condition even after relieving the load. We therefore speak of plastic material behaviour. The material subsequently undergoes strain-hardening and reaches its tensile strength at point B. However, failure of the material does not occur until point Z when the elongation at rupture is reached. The apparent reduction in stress is due to the reduction in the cross-sectional area ("necking"), which begins at point B.

Elastic modulus E
At 21 000 kN/cm², the elastic modulus is identical for all common structural steels. This corresponds to the slope of the stress-strain curve in the linear elastic range between points A and P.

Strain ε
Strain is the relationship between the change in length and the original length. When the yield point is reached, steel grade S235 exhibits a strain of 1.1%, whereas with grade S355 it is 1.7%. On the other hand, the strain of grade S235 at failure is 26% and that of grade S355 is only 22%!

Charpy V-notch impact test value
This value (in joules) depends on the temperature during testing and serves to assess the ductility and brittle fracture vulnerability of a steel.

Coefficient of thermal expansion α_T
This value specifies the elongation of a material exposed to temperature fluctuations. The coefficient of thermal expansion α_T for steel is 1.2×10^{-5} 1/K, which means that a steel beam 10 m long undergoes a 0.012% increase in length, i.e. 1.2 mm, for a temperature rise of 10 K. The compatibility of temperature fluctuations with the structure as a whole must always be checked and controlled by including expansion joints.

Further details of material properties can be found in the appendix (see pages 105–108).

to the desired surface finish quality and the durability. Further details about the use of stainless steel can be found in the chapter "Corrosion protection" (page 79); information on steel grades and alloys are given in the appendix

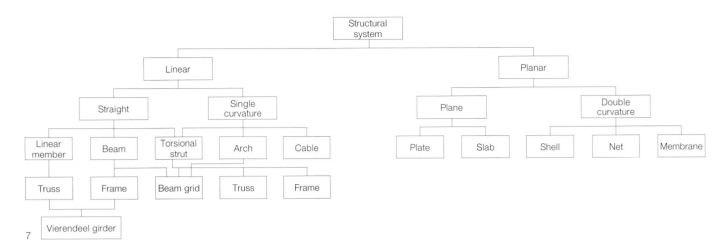

7

Structural systems, structural elements

An understanding of the structural action of basic structural systems forms the basis for their sensible inclusion individually and in combinations to form the complete loadbearing structure of a building. The most common structural elements are described below with respect to the way they carry the loads and the principles of their forms plus their design to suit structural steelwork. This compilation is deliberately limited to the most common loadbearing structures and the chief considerations, and does not claim to be exhaustive. The bibliography in the appendix suggests titles for further reading.
For a better understanding (and to serve as an overview), structural elements, some of which are listed in fig. 7, can be classified according to their form and main load-carrying action. This type of classification also describes, indirectly, the shape of the paths of the loads. Coupled with an understanding of the chief structural action, these paths form the basis for optimising the cross-sections and connection details for individual loadbearing elements and even whole loadbearing structures.

Structural steelwork design always involves an element of assembly. Therefore, as well as knowledge of the mechanical properties of the building material, the shaping and jointing options are equally important, which are described in the chapter "Assembling and connecting" (pages 45–63).
Construction with prefabricated and standardised sections, sheets and plates – known as differential construction – offers ideal conditions for creating economic structures. Besides the correct fabrication of the building components themselves, taking into account and detailing the load transfer points between the components is crucial. Load concentrations ensue at the connec-tions between, and supports, for structural elements, which in principle are associated with corresponding stress concentrations at these transitional points. Such stress concentrations are frequently critical for the design of the entire cross-section.

In structural steelwork, the differential form of construction also enables the simple jointing of elements made from different materials to form one building component. Here, knowledge about the flow of the forces in the loadbearing element is the basis for the sensible combination of steel with other building materials to form composite components.
Efficient composite structural elements are characterised by the fact that each material is used in a way best suited to its strengths and the stresses in the loadbearing element. At the same time, the combination of materials should result in synergies for the overall structure. For example, combining steel and concrete to form a composite column exploits the high load-carrying capacity of steel and the high fire resistance of concrete. But the large cross-sectional area of the concrete also increases the stiffness of the cross-section and improves the buckling stability.
During the conception of loadbearing structures, rough calculations taking into account the main effects are sufficient to provide initial dimensions for the components. After determining the loadbearing system, accurate calculations, prescribed by the codes of practice, are necessary for verifying adequate load-carrying capacity (stability) and serviceability. Verification of the ultimate loading capacity proves that a structure can resist the static and dynamic actions with a prescribed factor of safety both in terms of its individual parts and the structure as a whole.

Verification of the serviceability shows that the deformations caused by all the actions that could occur, as well as the vibration behaviour if applicable, lie within acceptable limits.

Knowledge of the structural relationships between the loadbearing elements with respect to load-carrying action is always associated with a reliable definition of the actions expected to occur. The most important structural systems are explained on the following pages.

7   Overview of structural systems (arranged according to form and load-carrying method)
8   Tree form as loadbearing structure
    Stuttgart Airport, 1981–91
    von Gerkan, Marg & Partner (GMP)
9   a "Linear member" loadbearing system showing deflected form
    b Buckling risk reduced through trussing
    c Buckling risk reduced by adjusting the cross-section
10 Deflected forms (deformation diagrams) and effective lengths of the Euler buckling cases depending on the type of support. The greater the effective length of a member, the greater is the risk of buckling for the same cross-section.

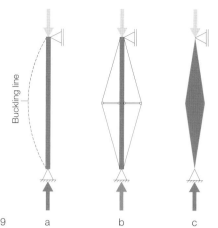

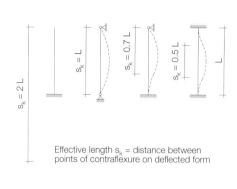

Effective length s_k = distance between points of contraflexure on deflected form

8
9   a   b   c
10

Linear member

The linear member, e.g. a bar in a truss or a prop beneath a beam, is the simplest structural element in a loadbearing structure.

In the structural analysis, the linear member is defined using the following geometric parameters: length (buckling length in the case of struts), cross-sectional area and second moment of the area. It is a straight component and carries tensile or compressive forces in the direction of the component axis, i.e. perpendicular to its cross-sectional area (normal or axial force). The tie, in contrast to the cable, is defined as having bending stiffness, which enables it to accommodate secondary bending moments due to self-weight, external loads or imperfections or eccentricities, without further assistance.

If the flow of forces in a structure is resolved into individual linear members such that the internal forces can be represented solely by axial forces, we speak of a truss.

In contrast to tension loads, compressive loads always give rise to a stability problem because the axis of the linear member tends to deviate from the straight line when subjected to compression. The resulting additional moments have to be taken into account in the design[1] (second-order theory). The analysis must show that the gradual deformations resulting from the additional moments steadily decrease.

Stability problems result in the following failure mechanisms depending on the shape of the cross-section:
• Global:
  Flexural buckling – buckling of the member axis
  Torsional-flexural buckling – buckling with simultaneous twisting of the member axis

• Local:
  Local buckling of a plate, possibly critical in cross-sections made up of thin plates, but not for rolled sections.

The form of the buckling depends primarily on the support conditions at the ends of the linear member, which may or may not permit any movement. Euler defined four buckling cases that cover a wide range of practical stability situations. If the support conditions are more complicated, the stability problem is generally solved by using a non-linear computer analysis based on the geometric imperfections of the construction.

In practical terms, it is possible to deal with the stability problem by adding lateral restraints to the section or by increasing the cross-sectional area and hence the radius of gyration. Increasing the radius of direction is achieved by shifting the cross-sectional area away from the centre of gravity as far as possible. If we consider the bending action resulting from the combination of axial compression and geometric imperfection, we can see that further optimisation is possible by adapting the shape of the cross-section to the shape of the bending moment diagram or by trussing the strut with cables. Compound linear members made up of individual sections connected with batten plates, or those designed as a truss, follow this optimisation principle. However, if the member forces are low, it should be remembered that the cost of fabrication is often far higher than the savings in weight and materials achieved through optimising the shape.

The optimum cross-sectional form for a strut with equal spacing of the lateral restraints against buckling at the ends of the member in all directions is therefore the doubly symmetric circular hollow section. As soon as the spacings of the buckling restraints for the various buckling planes differ or lateral loads, e.g. wind loads on facade posts, have to be carried, a singly symmetric cross-sectional form, e.g. a rectangular hollow section, is the best choice.

On the other hand, when sizing ties, the cross-sectional area is critical, irrespective of the distribution of the cross-sectional area or the limitation of elongation under maximum loading.

The basis for optimising ties, and struts especially, is early and careful planning of the details of supports and lateral restraints. Only then can the advantages of structural steelwork be exploited with respect to the shaping options for member cross-sections.

[1] DIN 18800 contains information on the theoretical inherent curvatures and eccentricities of linear member axes, e.g. due to imperfect fabrication (geometric imperfections) and deviations from the ideal material properties over the cross-section (structural imperfections).

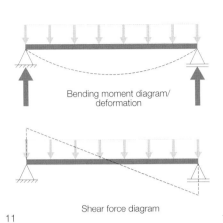

Bending moment diagram/
deformation

Shear force diagram

11

12

11 "Beam" loadbearing system showing bending
    moment and shear force diagrams
12 Beam for carrying roof loads
    "documenta" exhibition hall, Kassel, 1992
    Jourdan & Müller PAS

Beam

The beam is a linear loadbearing element that is mainly subjected to loads transverse to its axis, or to bending moments. The magnitude of the bending actions and their effects on a beam are best seen in the bending moment diagram. Moment actions can always be represented by a pair of opposing forces (couple) as well. In contrast to axial force actions on a linear member, the bending action on a beam leads to stresses that vary over the cross-section. Therefore, the use of the material varies correspondingly across the cross-section; zones of high and low tensile and compressive stresses are the result.

Owing to the poor use of the material when compared to axial force actions, bending actions on a cross-section represent the most inefficient form of loading. Loadbearing structures resolved into material-optimised individual members therefore follow the principle of the truss, where the external loads are carried without any bending, i.e. exclusively in the form of tensile and compressive forces.

Steel is a very efficient material for structures but is expensive when compared to many other building materials. The aim when designing steel structures, especially when optimising components and cross-sections subjected to bending, is therefore to maximise the stresses in relation to the cross-sectional area.
This shows why the I-section is so popular for beams in structural steelwork.

When optimising the cross-section and shape of a building component and carrying out the subsequent structural calculations, it is normally necessary to consider different load positions and combinations – the loading cases. This means there is a limit to the optimisation process

because different deflection curves and hence also different optimum forms (also varying along the length) result from the various loading cases. At the same time, the cost of an optimised form with a varying cross-section along the length of the beam must be taken into account because such beams are usually only economic above a certain tonnage of steel.

Let us first consider a beam cross-section subjected to pure bending. In this case the maximum tensile and compressive stresses occur at the edges with the greatest lever arm, measured from the axis of the member (fig. 13). Therefore, it is best to concentrate the material at these points. The bending stresses decrease to zero as we approach the axis of the member. The optimum cross-sectional form is therefore the I-section with a web whose thickness diminishes towards the member axis. Essentially, this shape serves to resist the force couple of tension and compression forces.
However, besides pure bending stresses, shear forces also occur in a beam, and certainly in a concentrated form at the supports. Shear forces are internal forces that act transverse to the axis of the member. They are resisted and carried almost entirely by the web. It is therefore primarily the magnitude of the shear forces that determines the thickness of the web and the need for additional stiffeners at positions of concentrated loading.

The bending moment normally varies along the length of the beam. When using I-section beams, this fact can be taken into account by welding additional plates to the flanges. However, as the addition of plates frequently leads to constructional problems owing to the changing level of the top flange, a good alternative is to use a welded plate girder with a changing flange thickness but where the

top of the top flange is at a constant level. Instead of adapting the cross-section of the components in order to handle non-constant loads on a loadbearing element subjected to bending, it is of course also possible to adjust the overall depth of the component to suit the varying load. One way of doing this is to use a haunched beam. The shape and length of the haunches should correspond to the bending moment diagram. Nevertheless, a beam of constant depth will still be necessary in some places in order to avoid cutting extreme feather edges, and to keep the fabrication work within reasonable economic constraints.

As the web carries the shear forces, this means that openings in the web, e.g. for services, can only be cut in zones with acceptably low shear forces, i.e. not in the region of supports or concentrated loads. If openings in these regions are unavoidable or if they exceed a certain size, then additional stiffeners must be included around the edges of the openings. Rounded corners to the openings should in any case be preferred to square ones in order to prevent stress peaks and the associated risk of cracking.

The aim of the structural analysis of beam sections is to ensure that the permissible stresses of the grade of steel used are not exceeded at any point in the cross-section under the most unfavourable loading cases and taking into account appropriate factors of safety.
As large areas of the beam cross-section are subjected to compressive stresses (see fig. 13), this results in a stability problem like in the strut. This problem can occur well before reaching the permissible stresses for material.
The risk of torsional-flexural buckling, in which the beam flange in compression deflects sideways and so twists the axis

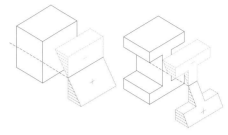

13 Comparison of the weight, load-carrying capacity, deformation and bending stress diagrams for
an I-section and a solid rectangular section with
the same overall dimensions (+ tension; - compression)
14 Development of loadbearing structures based on
the internal flow of forces (distribution of primary
stresses), in this case using the example of a
beam subjected to a uniformly distributed load.

	IPE 300	150 x 300
Weight	100 %	836 %
Load-carrying capacity	100 %	404 %
Deformation	100 %	207 %

13

of the beam, is a problem for deep and slender beams in particular. The problem can be overcome either by using sections with higher shear and torsion stiffness, which are less susceptible to stability problems, or by providing lateral support in the form of secondary beams, floor plates or bracing (with structural connections to the beam).

Bending in beams always causes curvature of the member axis and hence corresponding deformations. The deformation limit for structural steelwork is usually span/300. However, the limiting value for a particular construction should be chosen to be compatible with the use of the structure and the adjacent components, e.g. facades, partitions.

The depth of a beam has a crucial influence on the deformation. The maximum permissible deformation is therefore critical for the design. The aim should be to select the depth and shape of a beam such that the load-carrying capacity of the steel is fully exploited while still keeping within the deformation limits.

The stiffness of a beam subjected to dynamic loads should be chosen such that the natural frequency of the construction does not lie within the frequency range of the exciting load, in order to avoid resonance and a build-up of oscillations. This problem often occurs in structural steelwork with slender, long-span suspended floor constructions, or with footbridges. The normal pace of pedestrians lies between 1.5 and 3 Hz. The type of construction used should therefore have a natural frequency > 3 Hz, if additional attenuation measures are to be avoided (for economic reasons). High natural frequencies can be achieved by enhancing the stiffness of the construction, e.g. by increasing the structural depth and reducing the span.

Fig. 14 shows just a few of the many possible forms for a single-span beam. Depending on the magnitudes and positions of the external loads, an almost infinite number of further truss variants is conceivable. When opting for a resolved construction, it must be remembered that the benefits of optimising the material and the associated reduction in weight will to some extent be offset by the increased cost of fabrication. Therefore, standard rolled sections with a higher self-weight are often chosen purely for reasons of cost, provided the loads and the architectural intentions permit this. One cost-effective alternative is to use castellated or cellular beams.

The choice of section when designing a resolved system essentially depends on the type of connections intended for the joints. Pairs of channels back-to-back are ideal as the chords when using bolted truss assemblies with gusset plates. Welded girders are better suited to I-sections or structural hollow sections. And when using circular hollow sections, it should be remembered that the round members can result in awkward cutting at the joints, works which is often too complicated for smaller fabricators. The highest degree of material optimisation is achieved when cables can be used for the linear members of a truss that are always in tension regardless of the loading case. The strains and corresponding deformations of the overall construction must be analysed for such minimised cross-sections.

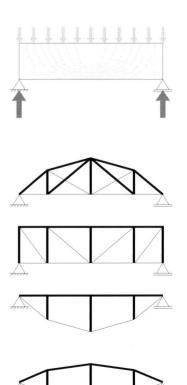

14

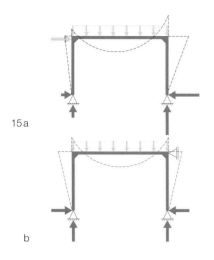

15a

b

16

15 "Frame" loadbearing system showing bending
   moment diagrams for
   a sway frame with horizontal load
   b non-sway frame, characterised by the upper
      horizontal restraint
16 Portal frame structure supporting the main span
   of a delicate bridge for pedestrians and cyclists
   Marina Bridge, Oberhausen, 1999
   netzwerkarchitekten
17 Redirecting the moments at the corner of a
   frame, showing a sensible stiffener arrangement

Frame

The frame is a structural system that results from the rigid connection of beam (cross-beam/rafter) and column (leg). This rigid connection, instead of a pinned connection, at the corner (knee) enables the support moment to be exploited, which means that the beam cross-section and the associated structural depth can be reduced, but the size of the column increases correspondingly. The provision of a rigid connection means that it is also possible to accommodate horizontal loads as well as vertical loads, which is why frames can be used to brace a structure.

Frames can be built in many structural forms: with fixed-base columns, or as one-, two- or three-pin structures. As the number of hinges increases, so the deformations of the frame, caused by external loads, also increase, but the restraint stresses due to settlement or temperature fluctuations, for example, decrease.
The hinges should be used for the on-site splices because there are no moments at these points and the forces to be transferred are correspondingly low. If this is not possible, the on-site splices should at least be in zones with low moments in order to keep these connections as simple as possible.

We distinguish between sway, braced and non-sway frames, which are braced in the horizontal direction by, for example, wind girders or floor plates. This distinction is not only critical for the nature and magnitude of the deformations caused by horizontal loads, but also for the effective lengths of the frame legs for buckling. The legs of non-sway frames are fixed at the cross-beam and therefore the effective length is shorter than the system length; the exact length depends on the stiffness of the cross-beam. In contrast to this, the effective length of the legs of

sway frames can be several times the system length.

Owing to the way they carry the loads (via bending), frames are inefficient constructions from the structural viewpoint. And from the economic viewpoint, they are therefore only justifiable up to certain spans or heights. For long spans and situations where there is ample depth available for the structure, it is more advisable to resolve the structure into a truss.

In the case of very long structures and long legs, it is sometimes better to refrain from using frames to provide the necessary bracing because the horizontal deformations can become excessive. The horizontal forces at roof and suspended floor levels can be resisted by horizontal wind girders positioned at strategic points, where the layout of vertical bracing elements (shear walls or girders) permits this. The best-known example of this type of stiffening is X-bracing between two pinned-end columns joined by a beam.
The rigid connection between cross-beam and leg has a decisive influence on the appearance of a frame. Axial forces, shear forces and bending moments have to be transferred across this joint. It should be remembered that in the case of I-sections and square/rectangular hollow sections the majority of the bending moment is carried via tensile and compressive forces in the flanges. The direction of action of these forces at the cross-beam/leg transition can only be changed by introducing another force. This additional force is normally cancelled out in the corner of the frame, but does lead to a high load in the web at this point which must be accommodated by stiffeners or by welding plates to the web.
The magnitude of the flange forces at the corner due to the bending moments can

be reduced by providing haunches at the ends of the cross-beam, which increases the lever arm.
Despite the high loads, erection splices are frequently positioned at the corners of the frame to ease the transport of the members. At such bolted connections, the flange forces are transferred to the bolts and that changes the lever arms accordingly. If the architectural requirements stipulate that the end plates should not protrude above the top flange of the cross-beam, the inclusion of a haunch at the corner is especially recommended.

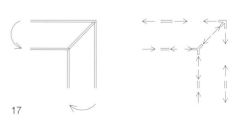

17

18

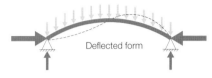

Deflected form

19

18 Two arches with a high rise within the plane of the facade carry the loads of the floors and enable the columns to be omitted on the ground floor
Broadgate Exchange House, London, 1989
SOM Architects
19 "Arch" loadbearing system showing snap-through buckling deflected form
20 Redirecting the external forces into axial forces through the curvature of the arch, sketch showing principle

Arch

The arch is normally a strut in the shape of a parabolic curve loaded both along its longitudinal axis and also transverse to this. The load transverse to the axis of the member is not carried via bending, like in a beam, but instead via axial forces (= normal forces, i.e. perpendicular to the plane of the cross-section), which result from the redirection of the forces due to the curvature of the member.
Carrying the external loads via axial forces in the loadbearing member makes the arch very efficient in terms of use of material. This phenomenon has already been explained in the "Beam" section (pages 36–37).

When subjected to a uniformly distributed load, the shape of the arch is similar to that of the bending moment diagram, i.e. a parabola. But if the critical loading on the arch is in the form of point loads, this gives rise to a so-called bar polygon, i.e. an arch consisting of straight members joining each load application point.
The optimum arch form for a particular loading case can be determined empirically with (suspended) catenary curve models, i.e. by first applying the loads to a cable (or chain) in tension. The form assumed by the cable when loaded is identical with the shape of the arch when reflected about the horizontal system axis. However, the form determined in this way corresponds to one loading case only, which means that all loads deviating from this particular loading case lead to bending in the arch. The use of an arch as a loadbearing element is therefore only advisable when there is one dominant loading case.

We must make a clear distinction between the arch as an architectural form and the arch as a loadbearing system. In the architectural sense, an arch is a curving

boundary to an opening, irrespective of the paths of the actions. And often this is merely a curved beam.

The compression load in the arch increases towards the supports, and a corresponding gradation of the section size, or the plate thicknesses if the overall dimensions of the section are to remain constant, is therefore advisable. The horizontal forces generated at the supports, the so-called thrust, must be resisted without significant deformations in the subsoil or the adjoining components of the structure. "Yielding" (i.e. sinking) supports lead to deformations in the arch and to bending as a result.
If the supports cannot resist the thrust, then cancelling this out by adding a tie between the supports is an alternative. Here, too, a tie with adequate strain stiffness is essential in order to limit the deformations in the arch. The magnitude of the axial forces occurring in the arch and the horizontal thrust at the supports depends on the span and the external loads as well as the rise of the arch itself; the greater the rise, the smaller is the horizontal thrust. As a rule, the horizontal thrust at a support is much higher than the vertical support reaction and consequently governs the design.

Arches can be rigid, i.e. constructed with fixed ends at the abutments, or built with one, two or three hinges. The number and positions of the hinges can be used to control the deformation behaviour and the bending moments due to moving loads. If vertical differential settlement of the subsoil is expected, a two-pin arch will reduce the restraint moments. If horizontal deformations occur at the same time, e.g. due to thrust, a three-pin arch is to be preferred.

As with a strut, stability is a critical factor in the design of arches. When checking the stability, lateral buckling in the plane of the arch should be investigated as well as the more familiar buckling perpendicular to the plane. In the former case the stability failure is in the form of so-called snap-through buckling (fig. 19).

Structural hollow sections are the best choice for steel arches because of their excellent buckling behaviour. Smaller members can be curved directly (cold- or hot-forming) to follow the shape of the arch, larger members are assembled from straight segments in the form of a polygon. At the joints, individual members can be connected by way of special castings, gusset plates or direct welding. The use of special castings does guarantee a perfect match between the node geometry and the path of a forces, but is expensive for small batches.

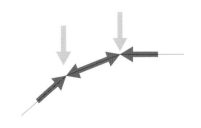

20

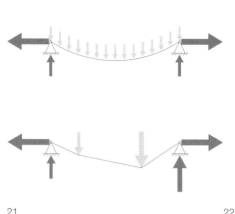

21

22

Cable

The cable is a purely tensile structural element. In contrast to the tie, a cable – at least for the sizes and cross-sections met with in structural engineering – has negligible bending stiffness. Whereas a tie can accommodate the external forces responsible for the tensile forces it has to carry at its ends only, a cable can carry loads acting transverse to its length and convert these into tensile forces through a "kink" in the course of the cable. A cable in such a situation could therefore be described as a polygon made up of ties. A cable in the sense of a loadbearing element can be made from solid material in the form of structural or prestressing steel, or as parallel-wire, strand or locked-coil cables made from wire rope. The different elastic moduli and strengths must always be taken into account. Owing to the exclusively tensile stresses, the cable is the most efficient loadbearing element from the point of view of material consumption. Every cable suspended from two points takes on a particular form for each loading case. Owing to its lack of bending stiffness, a cable will not carry any bending moments whatsoever. As the loading changes, so the sagging form of the suspended cable also changes. Catenary curve is the name given to the shape of a cable loadbearing structure in which the loads are carried without bending moments, i.e. exclusively via tensile forces. If another suspended loadbearing structure has the form of a catenary curve, or the catenary curve reflected about a horizontal line, then such a structure is not subjected to any bending moments, as already explained in the section on determining the optimum arch form.

The shape of the catenary curve depends entirely on the distribution of the loading. Point loads lead to kinks, uniformly distributed loads, e.g. due to self-weight, to parabolic curves, and combinations of the two to corresponding hybrid catenary curves.

A cable therefore exhibits considerable deformations as the load changes – changes that are incompatible with the serviceability requirements of structures. There are essentially two ways of solving this problem:

- Transfer the external loads into the cable via a stiffening beam which carries the loading cases deviating from the catenary curve via bending.
- Define and fix the catenary curve by prestressing the cable.

The prestress can be introduced with guy lines or kentledge. When using guy lines, then increasing the external loads or a minor change in the loading position does not lead to a different catenary curve, but instead simply to a reduction in the forces in the guy lines – in the extreme case even total slackening. For the kentledge option, the size of the kentledge should be chosen such that it is suitable for the catenary curve and additional loads result in only minor deformations.

This same principle is used for cable nets in double curvature which are used for delicate, long-span roofs: loadbearing cables for the primary span and guy lines in the other direction.

When designing and analysing cable structures, it is generally limiting the expansion and deformations that is critical as well as the load-carrying capacity. Owing to the delicate cross-sections of the cables themselves, detailing of the joints and intersections becomes very important. Welding, normally very popular for structural steelwork, cannot be used for joining cables – except when using structural steels with welded lugs and plates. The customary options for connecting cables are:

- cast elements
- forked ends and connecting plates or eye-bars
- clamping and pressing
- saddles

The connection systems or combinations thereof can be adapted to suit the requirements of a cable structure. But owing to the size of such connections, they do have a decisive influence on the appearance.

Looking at cable structures in terms of economics, it must be remembered during design and detailing that the cost of connecting the cables is, in comparison to the cables themselves, a critical cost factor. It is therefore important to maximise the length of the cable and minimise the number of joints, and also to simplify the connection principles.

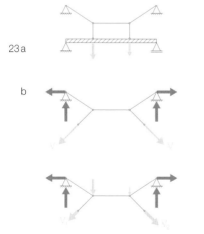

23 a

b

21   "Cable" loadbearing system
     The form of the catenary curve depends on the
     distribution of the loading.
22   Cable stabilised by stone deck
     Púnt da Surasuns, 1999, Conzett
     (see pages 90–91)
23   Cable stabilised by
     a stiffening beam
     b prestressing (V)

24

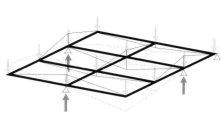

25

Beam grid

A beam grid consists of beams (with bending and torsional stiffness) in different directions joined together in one plane.

The loadbearing effect of a beam grid is similar to that of a slab resolved into a series of beams. As with a slab, a beam grid results in numerous options for supporting and positioning columns, which are dependent on the geometry of the intersections.

For a grid covering a large area, care should be taken to avoid all restraints when designing the supports by including appropriate measures to allow horizontal sway.

Normally, a beam grid consists of a series of beams intersecting at right-angles. Series of beams intersecting at acute angles involve more complicated fabrication – and are hence more expensive – and therefore are used only occasionally. The same is true for beam grids comprising three or more series of intersecting beams.

One special form is the beam grid with curved beams corresponding to the paths of the primary stresses (fig. 26). This grid form makes optimum use of the beam cross-sections, but more complicated connections are unavoidable.

Beam grids carry loads perpendicular to their system plane via the bending action in the series of beams. The distribution of the load over the individual beams depends on the ratio of the stiffnesses of the beam cross-sections and the ratio of the spans of the intersecting beams. We can assume that orthogonal beam grids with identical beam cross-sections in both directions exhibit a distinctive two-way spanning effect up to a span ratio of 1:1.5. As this span ratio increases, so a one-way spanning effect in the direction

of the shorter span becomes more and more evident. The series of beams with the longer span therefore gradually takes on the role of a secondary structure.

As already described in the "Beam" section, beam grids, too, can be optimised in terms of their material consumption by resolving the flow of forces. One way of doing this is to truss the series of beams from below. However, corresponding structural depths and more expense due to the processing of additional connections are the disadvantages.

A beam grid as the structural system for a steelwork construction may be chosen for the following reasons:
· The need for an adequate loadbearing system for a non-directional interior layout with exposed structural members.
· The need for an unhindered column layout through a closely spaced grid with good exploitation of the cross-sections.
· The need to minimise the structural depth as an alternative to a loadbearing system consisting of primary and secondary beams.

When selecting the beam cross-sections required for a beam grid, the details of the connections are just as critical as designing for load-carrying capacity and limiting the deformations, the usual criteria when designing members in bending.

The connections between the beams must be able to accommodate bending and torsion moments in addition to axial and shear forces. This increases the work and the cost of the construction at the connections, and is particularly true when the internal forces have to be transferred via bolted connections (i.e. on-site connections).

The use of welded connections enables the internal forces to be transferred more

harmoniously, but the types and sizes of weld seams must be checked with respect to their ease of execution (on-site connections, access between the beams).

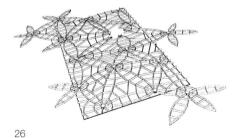

26

24 Beam grid cantilevering well beyond central columns
    Berlin National Gallery, 1968, Mies van der Rohe
25 "Beam grid" loadbearing system
    with bending moment diagram (thin line) and deformation (dotted line)
26 Beam grid form following the course of the primary loads on a point-supported slab
    Health clinic and thermal baths, Bad Colberg, 1997
    Kaufmann, Theilig & Partner

27

28a

b

c

27 Clear layout of interior and facade thanks to
    coordinated structural and interior design grids
    Magglingen sports hall, 1995–99, Max Schlupp
28 a Directional structure
    b Centred structures
    c Non-directional structures

Grids, geometrical arrangement

The question of the optimum grid for beams and columns must be decided for every construction project separately. The systematic arrangement of columns on a plan grid results in regular layouts for the loadbearing elements to suspended floors or roofs. The main reasons for this are economic considerations and easier planning due to the repetitive dimensions of basic components. At the same time, this approach ensures – for an identical structural depth – consistent and even deformations in the various bays of the grid when the structure is loaded. Furthermore, a consistent, lucid grid emphasizes the aesthetics of a frame construction.

The column positions are based on the following principal boundary conditions:
• plan layout dependent on use
• facade design
• position of points for load transfer or foundations
• limiting the structural depths

Possible column positions are initially investigated separately for interior and perimeter columns. Interior columns do not usually have an influence on the appearance of a building and are relatively easy to incorporate in the plan layout. The positions of the perimeter columns, on the other hand, have a direct influence on the appearance of the facade and the grid for internal finishes and fittings. One of three basic column layouts can be chosen:
• Widely spaced columns set back from the facade which allow corresponding freedoms for the design of the facade, but inevitably result in restrictions because of their placement within the interior space.
• Widely spaced columns integrated into the facade. This generally results in a vertical division of the facade because

the loadbearing columns are much larger than the posts supporting the facade.
Closely spaced columns in the facade. The columns carry lighter loads and their dimensions can therefore be similar to those of the facade posts, and the same types of section can be used. Facade elements can also be fixed directly to the columns and a separate supporting framework for the facade is then unnecessary.

The above boundary conditions for the choice of grid for the vertical construction elements can be used to develop the grid for the horizontal members. This is based on basic geometric forms that can be divided into directional, non-directional and centred loadbearing structures.

Directional orthogonal loadbearing structures are based on a rectangular grid and are always characterised by primary and secondary loadbearing directions; the path for the forces is hierarchical. The arrangement makes use of primary and secondary beams (primary and secondary structures).
When designing and sizing the beams, the first step is to establish whether the series of beams can be "stacked" one on top of the other, or positioned with their top edges/flanges flush. The advantage of stacking is that continuity effects, which make better use of constant sectional properties, can be achieved with little effort. However, the downside is that the overall construction is much deeper. In the flush arrangement, the continuity effect of the secondary beams, where they cross the main beams, can only be achieved with considerable additional work, and may therefore be undesirable, possibly also from the appearance point of view. To achieve optimum use of the available structural depth, it is usually

better to span the heavily loaded primary beams over a shorter distance than the more lightly loaded secondary beams. A loadbearing structure can be made more economic by shortening the paths over which the loads have to be transferred, and by reducing the number of elements involved in the load transfer. The upshot of this is that a primary structure with load-carrying members in one direction and the infilling material (floor, roof) at right-angles to this is the most economic solution. However, the introduction of secondary and, if required, tertiary structures enables correspondingly larger spans to be achieved.

In non-directional loadbearing structures, the loads are carried more or less evenly in at least two directions. Beam grids or space structures based on square or triangular layouts are necessary for this. Carrying the load as evenly as possible in all directions is, however, only possible with a suitable uniform grid based on squares or equilateral triangles.

Centred loadbearing structures represent a special type of grid. Generally, centred grids are formed over loadbearing elements that are aligned with the centre of a circle or the focal points of an ellipse.

Besides the considerations concerning span, load-carrying efficiency, architecture and arrangement of the grid, questions regarding the routing of services and the type of infilling (walls, floors, roofs) must be sensibly answered when determining the grid.

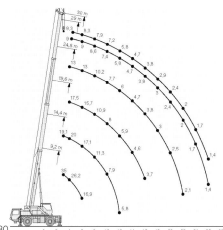

29 Erecting structural steelwork (BIG 3) on the
    Tiefenbachkogel mountain, Austria
30 Lifting capacities related to jib length for a 35 t
    mobile crane
31 Permissible dimensions and total weights for
    loaded road transport vehicles

Transport and erection

Just like the load-carrying aspects of the structure itself, transport and erection matters also have an influence on the design of steel structures and their details.

The industrial prefabrication of the steel components itself involves numerous transport processes whose limits in terms of weight and dimensions are heavily dependent on the facilities of the particular fabricator. Early consideration of the boundary conditions in the fabrication works and on the building site therefore guarantees a sensible breakdown of the overall construction into individual parts or subassemblies and the appropriate detailed design.

Planning of the fabrication work, which normally takes place in the engineering office of the steel fabricator, involves adjusting the requirements of the architect and the structural engineer to suit the specific boundary conditions of the production and the construction sequence. This can lead to considerable deviations from the intended appearance of the construction and the load-carrying intentions. Therefore, fabrication drawings must always be checked and approved by the design team, and aspects important to the architecture, e.g. type of section, type of connection, precisely defined beforehand in the specification.

Various factors have to be taken into account when deciding on the most economic form of transport. In particular, it should be remembered that there is an interaction between the size of a component for transport after completion of fabrication in the works and the lifting equipment available on the building site. Different solutions should therefore always be investigated for the transport and erection procedures.

The limitations in terms of maximum dimensions and permissible weights

placed on road transport by the applicable road traffic laws generally define the feasibility and economics with respect to the size of individual elements of the construction.

Owing to the high degree of prefabrication, which even includes the application of corrosion protection media, subsequent changes to components already delivered to the building site are very restricted and are associated with considerable work (and costs) and a drop in quality. Therefore, detailed, careful planning, right up to defining the lifting points and the lifting plant, is vital in structural steelwork. Ideally, components delivered to the building site should be placed directly below or adjacent to the lifting equipment and lifted into place on the structure without intermediate storage.

A minimum number of identical bolts (diameter, grade) should be used for on-site bolted connections in order to minimise erection work and prevent incorrect bolting. On-site welding should be avoided whenever possible. If welding is unavoidable, the advice of a specialist welding engineer should be sought when planning and determining the grades of steel to be

used. Taking into account and limiting the building tolerances to DIN 18201, DIN 18202 and DIN 18203 are critical when planning erection sequences. It is essential to make sure that the permissible tolerances can be accommodated without generating restraint stresses within the structure. On the building site, the precision possible in the prefabrication of steel components frequently conflicts with the lower accuracy of components made from reinforced concrete or timber. Therefore, significant dimensional inaccuracies at the interfaces between structural steelwork and other trades must always be considered and allowed for in the planning. This applies particularly to the (concrete) foundations to steel components.

Besides taking into account erection sequences, it is often also necessary to plan for the dismantling of the structure when designing structural steelwork. Detachable clamped and bolted connections at on-site splices and good access to connections will render possible dismantling. Possible wear in the connections in the case of repetitive dismantling and re-erection should be allowed for in the design.

Permissible dimensions and total weights for loaded road transport vehicles according to cl. 32 and 34 of the German Road Traffic Act

	Road transport without special approval				Heavy and special vehicles	
	vehicle with 2 axles	vehicle with > 2 axles	tractor + trailer	truck + trailer	with annual approval	with individual approval
Length [m]	12.00	12.00	15.50[1]	18.00	25.00	> 25.00
Width [m]	2.50	2.50	2.50	2.50	3.00	> 3.00
Height [m]	4.00	4.00	4.00	4.00	4.00	> 4.00
Total weight [t]	16.00	22.00	40.00	40.00	40.00[2]	> 40.00

[1] 16.50 m to Euronorm
31 [2] 42.00 t for indivisible loads

Assembling and connecting

The various parts of the loadbearing structure need to be assembled to form the complete construction. Those parts then have a mutual influence on each other and act together to form a whole. The term "assembly" can be broken down into the various facets of the construction of loadbearing structures:
- The assembly of individual components to form one loadbearing element, e.g. lattice girders, compound beams, compound columns.
- The assembly of loadbearing elements to form loadbearing structures, e.g. foundation + column + beam + floor.
- The assembly of loadbearing structures to form complete constructions, e.g. steel frame + reinforced concrete core, structure + facade.

The most important criteria for assembling the parts of the structure are:
- The material: parameters and properties.
- The flow of forces: internal and external forces should be transmitted in a direct way and with the minimum of effort.
- The geometry: geometry and optimum flow of forces are mutually dependent; intersections and penetrations require special attention (appropriate cross-sectional forms and sensible configuration of loadbearing elements).
- The fabrication, processing and erection: methods of production and degree of prefabrication.
- The means of connection: the choice depends on the respective material, the loads and the flow of forces (the structural system), the fabrication and erection.
- The form: the structural system selected, the materials used and the connecting of the loadbearing parts determines the appearance of the loadbearing structure.

In terms of the overall concept of the loadbearing structure and the arrangement of the details, the form of assembly has a decisive influence on the appearance of the finished structure. Well-proportioned connections that render visible the flow of forces, coordinated choice of sections for columns, beams and further subsystems and their clear geometrical allocation can lend the structure a high aesthetic quality. The conception of an efficient loadbearing structure and the careful arrangement of its details not only calls for engineering skills, but also gives the architect numerous design freedoms. The most important principles for assembling and connecting loadbearing components made from steel are presented on the following pages.

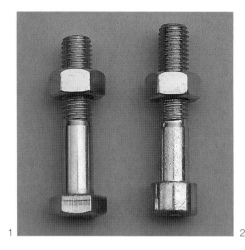

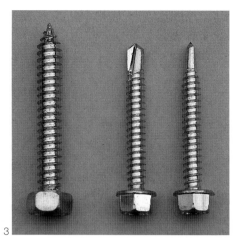

1

2

3

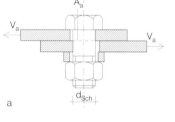

4   a

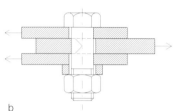

b

DIN 6901   DIN 7971   DIN 7972   Din 7973

5   DIN 7976   DIN 7981   DIN 7982   Din 7983

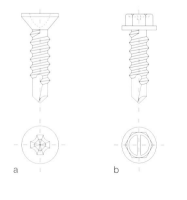

6   a   b

7 a   b   c   d   e   f

Means of connection

Bolts and screws

Bolts and screws are among the most important types of fasteners used in structural steelwork. The advantages of screwed or bolted connections are:

- ease of handling on the building site and in the works,
- excellent availability of bolts and screws in various qualities and strengths,
- easy removal if necessary – an important prerequisite for the dismantling and re-erection of steel components.

The use of screwed or bolted connections in structural steelwork opens up numerous options. Structural connections between plates and rolled sections can be achieved with the most diverse fasteners, with or without nuts and washers. Hexagon-head bolts in standard or close-tolerance forms plus countersunk-head bolts with hexagon socket are approved for structural connections. Depending on the material of the bolt (strength grade), we can also distinguish between standard and high-strength bolts. Bolts can be loaded in tension or in shear or a combination of both.

The abbreviated form of the bolt designation is made up as follows:

- bolt type designation (e.g. close-tolerance bolt)
- type of thread (M = metric thread)
- bolt diameter (in mm)
- bolt material (e.g. high-strength: 10.9)

The layout of the bolts at a connection can turn out to be a distinctive design feature and should be decided on jointly by the architect and the structural engineer. It may prove necessary to screw bolts into threaded holes for architectural or constructional reasons, which means that nuts are not required.

When connecting thin sheet metal and facade components, self-drilling screws (which drill their own hole) or self-tapping screws (which tap their own thread in a pre-drilled hole) are often employed. Such screws do not require nuts.

Rivets

Riveting creates a non-detachable connection between parts of the structure with the help of an upset fastener, the rivet.

Owing to the excessive noise and the labour-intensive hard work, the traditional (solid) rivet has these days been almost exclusively relegated to the repair of (older) riveted constructions. The newer, easy-to-use pop rivets are used in the building industry mainly for fastening thin sheet metal components. Pop rivets, which require access from one side only,

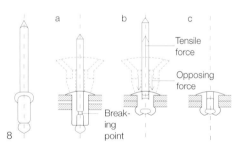

8

1   Left: hexagon-head bolt; right: stainless steel close-tolerance bolt with hexagon socket
2   Vierendeel girders made from steel plates, with precise bolting arrangement
3   Left: self-tapping screw; right: self-drilling screws
4   Hexagon-head bolt with metric thread
     a   bolted connection in single shear
     b   bolted connection in double shear
5   Self-tapping screws for sheet metal
6   Self-drilling screws
     a   crosshead countersunk
     b   with hexagon washer head and screwdriver slot
7   Typical rivet forms
     a   round (DIN 660)
     b   large round (DIN 663)
     c   countersunk (DIN 661)
     d   half-round (DIN 632)
     e   mushroom (DIN 674)
     f   extra wide for belts (DIN 675)
8   Operations for inserting a pop rivet

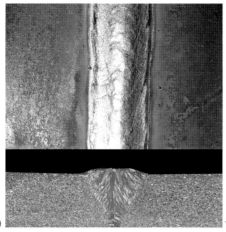

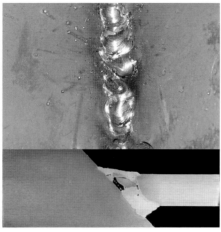

9 Good quality weld seam, elevation and section
10 Poor quality weld seam, elevation and section
11 Types of joint, forms and dimensions of weld
   seams to DIN 18800-1
   [1] to DIN 18800-7, section 3.4.3

Cross-sectional forms of weld seams

	No.	Symbol	Type of seam[1]	Diagram
Welds without root penetration	1		V-groove butt joint	t_1 ... t_2
	2		Double bevel T-joint	t_2 ... t_1
	3		Bevel T-joint	with backing run — t_2, backing run, t_1
	4		Bevel T-joint	with root penetration — t_2 ... t_1
Welds with root penetration or sealing runs	5		J-groove T-joint with fillet	with backing run if required — a, t_2, $\leq 60°$, t_1
	6		J-groove butt joint	a, $\leq 60°$
	7		Double bevel T-joint with fillets	a, t_1, a, t_2, $\leq 60°$
	8		Double J-groove butt joint	a, a
Fillet welds	9		Square butt joint without joint preparation (fully automatic weld)	b, t_1, a, c
	10		T-joint with fillet	theoretical root — t_1, a, t_2
	11		T-joint with double fillet	theoretical root — t_1, a, t_2

11

are especially useful when working with hollow sections.

Welding
Welding, alongside screws/bolts, is the other standard form of connection in structural steelwork. Welding involves fusing together two or more identical or very similar steels to form one homogeneous component, and this is done by melting them together at their interface through liquefaction or plastic deformation. This can be carried out with or without the addition of another material. The following fusion welding processes are important for structural steelwork:
· arc welding
· shielded metal-arc welding
· flash butt welding
· oxyacetylene welding
The geometry and function of the parts to be joined in the welded construction determine the type of joint and the form of the weld seam. When designing the joint, care should be taken to ensure complete root penetration and fusion of the flanks of the joint, taking into account the type of weld selected. When specifying the form of the weld seam, a reference sample should be agreed with the welding contractor in order to guarantee the desired appearance.
Weld seams in structural steelwork may only be carried out by appropriately trained welders. If necessary, the weld seams can be inspected at the request of the checking engineer by specialists who can use x-rays and ultrasound methods to investigate the toughness, strength, deformation capacity and flaws in the material. A special aspect of on-site weld seams is the subsequent application of corrosion protection coatings.

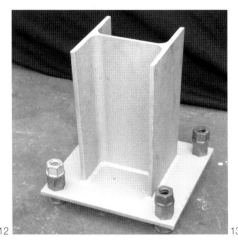

12 13 14

Columns

One-piece columns
The main applications for steel in the construction industry are linear loadbearing elements such as columns and beams. Columns (often called stanchions in structural steelwork) transfer the loads from the suspended floors and the roof to the foundations. They can be designed with pinned or fixed ends. The high strength of steel leads to slender cross-sections whose stability behaviour must be given special attention (see also page 35). The risk of buckling is avoided by choosing suitable cross-sections and/or by adding stiffeners. As the axis of a column can buckle in any direction, rotationally symmetric cross-sections such as circular hollow sections are especially suitable where buckling is critical. But if a column is prevented from buckling about one axis, then a singly symmetric cross-section, e.g. a rectangular hollow section or a slender I-section, is a good choice. The increasing loads from top to bottom in multi-storey structures can be accommodated within the column cross-section, without altering the overall dimensions, simply by increasing the wall/web/flange thicknesses or the grade of steel. Both hollow and rolled sections enable the easy vertical routing of building services; however, care should be taken to ensure that any holes necessary do not weaken the cross-section. The cross-sections most frequently used for columns in compression are:
• structural hollow sections
• wide-flange beams of the HE series
• welded hollow sections
• compound sections

Compound and resolved columns
Columns can also be assembled from individual sections and/or plates to suit particular conditions. Batten or lacing

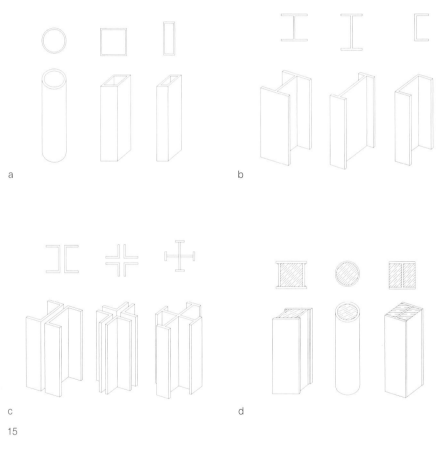

a

b

c

d

15

pieces are used to join together identical sections with a defined, constant spacing to form one column.

In order to avoid wasting material, it is advisable to adjust the cross-sections of very tall columns to suit the loading. This can be done, for example, by resolving

the cross-section into a multi-chord truss- or frame-like column. In the case of pinned-end columns, the chords can be brought together at the top and bottom to form an obvious "pin", or all chords can be taken down to the foundation to create a simple fixed base. Compound columns

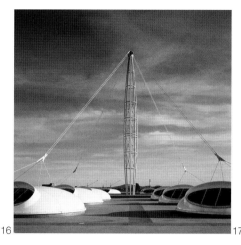

16   17

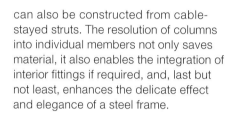

12 Typical welded connection between column and
    base plate to spread the load
13 Roof beam-column connection,
    Berlin National Gallery, 1968,
    Ludwig Mies van der Rohe
14 Composite column (open steel section + con-
    crete infill between flanges)
15 a Hollow sections
    b Open rolled sections
    c Compound columns
    d Composite columns (steel + concrete)
16 Pylon column in the form of a lattice mast with a
    round cross-section, factory building, Cologne,
    1992, Nicholas Grimshaw
17 Cable-stayed columns, Renault Distribution
    Centre, Swindon, UK, 1982, Norman Foster
18 Compound three-chord lattice column made from
    welded circular hollow sections with diagonal
    bracing
19 Compound four-chord lattice column made from
    hollow sections with rigid welded joints

18   19

can also be constructed from cable-
stayed struts. The resolution of columns
into individual members not only saves
material, it also enables the integration of
interior fittings if required, and, last but
not least, enhances the delicate effect
and elegance of a steel frame.

Composite columns
The load-carrying capacity and the fire
resistance of an exclusively steel column
can be improved by the addition of plain
or reinforced concrete. Provided the concrete cover to the steel section and the
steel reinforcement is adequate and additional longitudinal reinforcing bars are
included, composite columns can be
allocated to a very high fire resistance
class. Open steel sections with a concrete filling between the flanges are frequently used because they are very easy
to build and the steel flanges remain visible, which allows other steel items (loadbearing or otherwise) to be welded to
them afterwards.
The possible gain in load-carrying capacity of a concrete-filled hollow section is in
the same order of magnitude as an open
section with a concrete filling between the
flanges. If concrete-filled hollow sections
are reinforced with additional steel sections, then even further gradations of
load-carrying capacity are possible while
retaining the same overall dimensions –
especially important for multi-storey
columns.

20   21   22

Beams

Solid-web beams

When designing a component subjected to bending (see pages 36–38), the form and the cross-section should be arranged in such a way that maximum possible utilisation of the material is achieved. In structural steelwork, I-sections or hollow box beams are preferred for members subjected to bending. Openings in the webs, e.g. for pipes and cables, should preferably be circular or have rounded corners and should be positioned only in regions with low shear forces, i.e. not in the direct vicinity of supports, for instance. As the webs of castellated and cellular beams are weakened over their full length, they must be looked at critically where high shear forces occur and may need to be stiffened locally. Instead of dealing with bending stresses by adjusting the cross-section and maintaining a constant depth, in most cases it is much more efficient to adjust the depth of the beam itself to the loading situation.

Compound and resolved beams

If we increase the depth of a beam and its openings such that only bar-type regions remain, we have created the transition to a resolved cross-section – a lattice beam or Vierendeel girder. The risk of torsional-flexural buckling must be considered for such deep, slender members in bending (see page 37). The Vierendeel girder, named after the Belgian engineer Arthur Vierendeel, normally consists of two parallel chords linked by vertical struts. Owing to the lack of diagonals, the joints must be designed as rigid and such girders are markedly heavier than equivalent lattice beams. However, Vierendeel girders offer plenty of scope for routing services, and their clean lines lend them a high aesthetic quality.

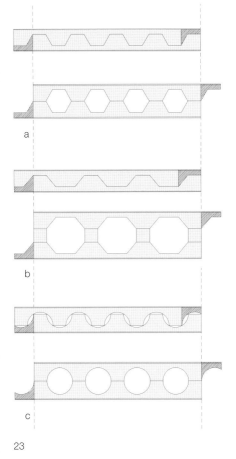

a

b

c

23

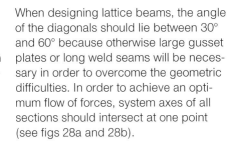

When designing lattice beams, the angle of the diagonals should lie between 30° and 60° because otherwise large gusset plates or long weld seams will be necessary in order to overcome the geometric difficulties. In order to achieve an optimum flow of forces, system axes of all sections should intersect at one point (see figs 28a and 28b).

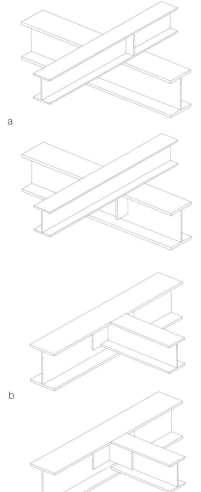

a

b

24

20   Production of cellular beams
21   Dome supported on three-chord trusses, Märker circular mixed bed, Harburg, 2000, Ackermann & Partner
22   Beyeler Collection, Riehen, 1997, Renzo Piano
23   a–b Production of a castellated beam from an I-section without (a) and with (b) intermediate web plates
     c   Patented method for producing a cellular beam from one I-section
24   a   Assembling primary and secondary beams continuous in two layers, with space for building services
     b   Assembling primary and secondary beams in one layer with pinned connections – the reduced structural depth is advantageous

25

26

27

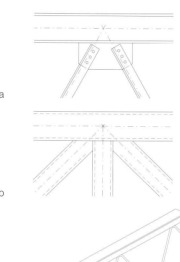

28

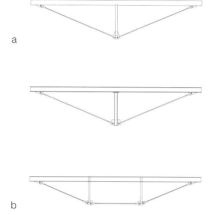

a

b

c

d

29

Examples of beams made up of steel sections:

- Lattice beams with chords made from T-sections, halved I-sections or circular hollow sections, diagonals made from solid round sections in the form of individual bars or a continuous vertical "wave".
- Lattice beams made from steel angles with gusset plates: chords made from two angles back to back, diagonals from one or two angles, with bolted or welded connections.
- Lattice beams with chords made from T-sections and diagonals from angles, pairs of angles or channel sections.
- Lattice beams with varying infill bars: vertical struts made from angle sections with good buckling properties, diagonal ties (rising towards the supports) made from steel flats.
- Lattice beams made from circular hollow sections: wall thicknesses can be adjusted to suit the loads while retaining the same outside diameter, welded connections.

Combinations of beam systems
In structural steelwork, the design engineer has almost infinite possibilities at his disposal when devising beam systems; the only limits are those imposed by his own fantasy. The aforementioned I-sections, lattice beams and Vierendeel girders can be combined with trussing systems above and below the beams to achieve longer spans without compromising the lightness and delicateness of the load-bearing structure. The use of single and multiple trussing systems below the beam, or trussing systems above the beam, right up to suspended and cable-stayed constructions, enable spans to be achieved that are impossible with other materials.

25 Single-span beams in the form of three-chord trusses, Hamburg Airport, 1993, GMP
26 Vierendeel girders with suspended purlins, ice rink, Munich, 1991, Ackermann & Partner
27 Trussed pairs of curved IPE sections, factory building, Saint-Quentin-en-Yvelines, 1991, Renzo Piano
28 a Bolted lattice beam connection, with simple gusset plate
   b Lattice beam made from rectangular hollow sections, connection of verticals and diagonals to top chord
   c Lattice beams made from combinations of various steel sections
29 a, b Trussed beams
   c Trussed beam in fish-belly form
   d Polenceau truss

30

31

32

Column base

When transferring the compressive forces into the foundation, it must be remembered that the concrete cannot usually accept the direct transmission of forces because the concentrated load would be too high. The forces in the steel column are therefore transferred to the concrete via a base plate which spreads the load. The thickness of the base plate should be sufficient to prevent deformations such as lifting of the corners. Instead of a thick base plate, a thinner plate with stiffeners between column and plate to distribute the load is also feasible.

A sufficiently large joint should be included between the underside of the base plate and the top of the concrete foundation in order to accommodate the inevitable on-site inaccuracies. During erection, shims or packing pieces are placed under the base plate to achieve the correct level of the structural steelwork, and the remaining gap is then filled with a non-shrink grout. If prefabricated flooring units are to be installed, a clean junction at the base of the column is important. Open sections should be closed off with welded plates at the base, or changed to hollow/box sections (see, for example, page 97). If the loads are only low, the base plate can be attached to the foundation with expanding or resin anchors. In the case of higher loads and fixed-end columns, anchors plus cast-in steel sections will be necessary. Threaded bars and holding-down bolts are positioned accurately within the formwork by means of templates and then cast into the foundation. This arrangement is intended to ensure correct and accurate positioning, and corrections at a later date are extremely difficult and costly to correct. In the case of refurbishment projects and additional columns at a later date, the base plates can be fixed with expanding or resin anchors.

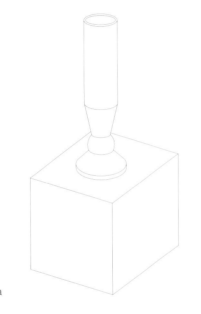

a

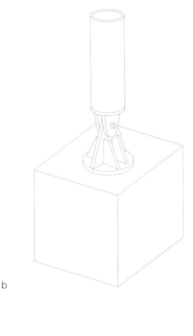

b

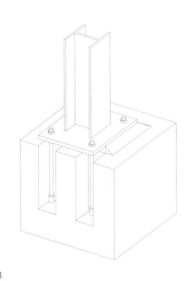

c

33

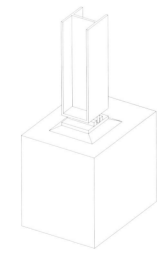

d

30 Column base detail allowing rotation in one
    direction
31 Steel corner column on clay brick foundation,
    IIT Navy Building, Chicago, 1947,
    Ludwig Mies van der Rohe
32 Column base with plate to spread the load and
    grouting allowance

33 a Column base detail with ball joint allowing
       rotation in two directions
    b Column base detail with stiffened plate allow-
       ing rotation in one direction
    c Fixed column base with anchor bolts
    d Pinned column base with cleat support

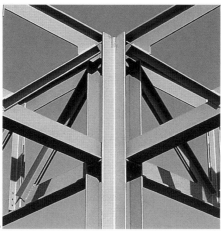

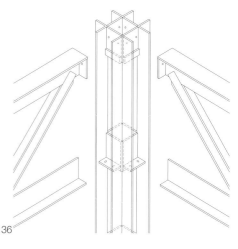

34

35

36

Column-beam connection

Connections between columns and beams are initially an engineering problem, facing questions of transfer of forces, fabrication and erection. However, if the steelwork is to remain exposed, then the designer must satisfy considerable aesthetic demands as well. These include coordinating the geometry of the column and beam cross-sections, revealing the flow of the forces and refraining from developing too many different connection details for one structure.

In principle, we distinguish between pinned and rigid connections. Rigid frame corners can be achieved with either bolts or welding. But with bolted connections care should be taken to ensure that the high bending forces do not lead to unwieldy, excessively large connections. Erection splices should therefore be positioned at hinges or places with low bending moments. Three-dimensional column-beam systems with pinned joints must be braced with diagonals and wind girders. These are classed as (trussed) plates. This is the most common type of construction used in structural steelwork and, owing to the lack of bending actions, is far superior to rigid frame construction. The amount of material required is considerably reduced and the connections are much simpler. Connections are usually bolted and therefore can be easily handled on the building site. The jointing options for bolted connections between beams and columns can be achieved via end plates, folded plates or web cleats. Another assembly variation is to carry the vertical load via a seating cleat beneath the beam.

a

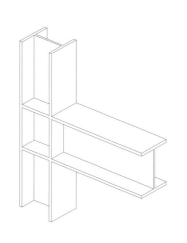

b

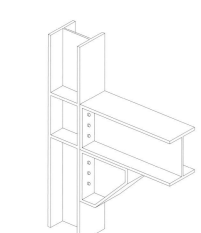

c

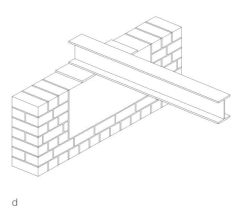

d

37

34 Special cast joint connecting different column cross-sections and floor beams, office building, Bedfont Lakes, 1992, Michael Hopkins
35 Compound column supporting lattice beams, MAXI steel building system, 1962-94, Fritz Haller
36 Column-lattice beam connection, isometric view not to scale, MAXI steel building system

37 a Beam-column connection with bolts to secure joint in position and stiffeners to transfer shear forces
    b Rigid column-beam-column connection, welded
    c Rigid column-beam-column connection, bolted
    d Steel beam supported on masonry with spreader plate to transfer forces

Bracing

Structures must be braced for stability purposes (imperfections) and to accommodate horizontal loads (wind). Steel frames can be very effectively braced with girders, i.e. plates resolved into truss-like constructions. To do this, at least three vertical girders are required, positioned on plan such that their system axes do not intersect at one point. The load is transferred into and out of these girders normally by way of horizontal girders in the plane of the roof or a suspended floor. However, plates or frames may be used instead of such girders. Wind girders with diagonals disrupt the unrestricted use of a building and therefore they are positioned in the plane of the facade or in permanent walls to access or service cores. The diagonals are connected to the beams and columns by means of gusset plates or direct welding. When designing the details, attention should be given to the fact that the designer's hinge assumptions at the joints are not always realised in practice. Bolted or welded joints can introduce bending stresses into the individual bars via the gusset plates. However, these secondary stresses can be ignored in the case of diagonals with adequate slenderness ratios.

We distinguish between diagonals that can accommodate tensile and compressive forces, and those that can accommodate tensile forces only, and therefore are not at risk of buckling. In principle, all components with a constant cross-section and straight member axis are suitable as ties, but cables or solid round sections are particularly good at expressing the purpose of such structural elements. Both cables and tie bars can be connected to the adjoining components via approved, aesthetically pleasing fittings, although tie bars can also be connected via simple and inexpensive welded gusset plates. Cables have a much higher strength than solid bars and can accommodate higher loads. However, they are considerably more expensive and must be prestressed during erection in order to prevent the cable from sagging.

The lengths of tie bars provided with left- and right-hand threads at opposite ends can be easily adjusted on site by screwing them into matching end fittings.

38

39

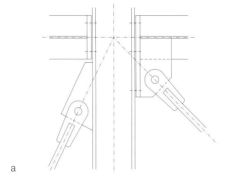

a

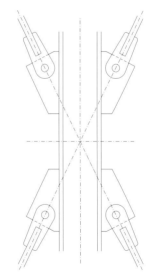

b

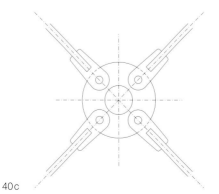

40c

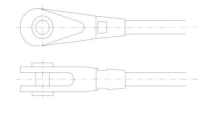

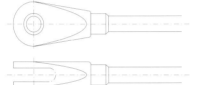

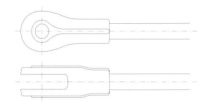

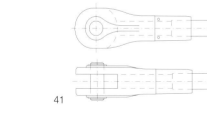

41

38 Vertical wind girder in plane of facade,
   Valeo wipers plant, Beitigheim-Bissingen, 2002,
   Ackermann & Partner
39 CIM Institute, Braunschweig, 1992,
   Schulitz + Partner
40 Examples of bracing details
   a connection of diagonals to column-beam joint
   b connection of X-bracing at intermediate
   column
   c intersection of X-bracing members
41 Ties with different types of screwed end fitting
42 Examples of connection principles for open steel
   sections

Vierendeel girders made from bolted steel plates

The architects and engineers on this project worked together to devise a roof structure that would span over different internal uses in a training centre. Clean lines were called for that would not disturb the concentration of users. The result was a construction made from rolled sections that could be adapted to the needs of the various building services plus Vierendeel girders to support the fully glazed roof over the general assembly area where students congregate between training sessions.

The primary structure, on a 5 m grid, consists of pinned-end columns and main beams made from rolled sections. The secondary structure comprises secondary beams on a 2.5 m grid (which is better for the services) for supporting the roof covering of trapezoidal profile sheeting. The building services are suspended from these secondary beams and at the same time the beams also provide lateral restraint to the main beams.

The columns (HEB 180 sections) stand on strip footings, side walls or reinforced concrete piers and carry the main beams (IPE 500 sections). The columns are fixed at the base in order to guarantee adequate stability during the construction period before the roof plate was built. In the final condition, the roof plate together with the shear walls ensures the stability of the building.

The glazed roof over the central bay of the building is supported on Vierendeel girders spanning 10 m. These girders are made up of two 15 mm thick plates, 720–870 mm deep, that are bolted together at a defined spacing ensured with spacer sleeves. The secondary beams provide the necessary lateral restraint.

All connections are bolted. The roof plate is formed by horizontal girders made from solid round sections. Five reinforced concrete cores, to which the structural steelwork is attached, stabilise the construction.

The cross-sections are mainly fabricated from steel grade S 235 JR G2 (formerly RSt 37-2). To achieve a higher loadbearing capacity and also better fire resistance, the columns are filled with concrete between the flanges at ground floor level.

1   During construction
2   BMW Training Academy, Unterschleissheim near Munich, 2004
    Architects: Ackermann & Partner
    Structural engineer: Christoph Ackermann

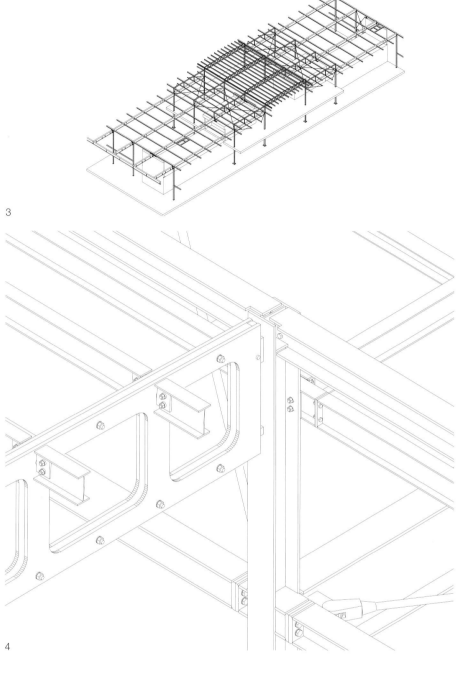

3

3 Isometric view of structural system
4 Connection of Vierendeel girder to primary
   structure
5 Girder-column connection, scale 1:20
6 Section through Vierendeel girder showing
   expansion joint arrangement and horizontal
   wind girder, scale 1:20

4

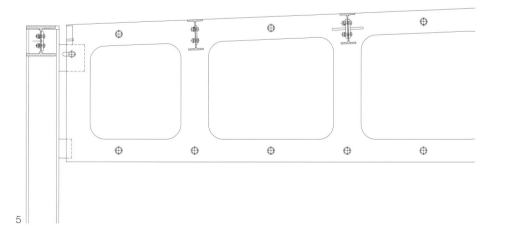

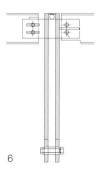

5

6

7

External lattice beams with suspended secondary beam system

The roof to this industrial shed is supported by an external loadbearing structure from which the system of secondary beams is suspended. Stability of the building is ensured by internal reinforced concrete cores, stairs and ventilation plant rooms.

The primary structure consists of lattice beams made up of open steel sections. This construction is positioned outside the building envelope in order to comply with urban planning stipulations regarding a low eaves height – to fit in with the small-scale neighbouring buildings – and also to reduce the building volume requiring conditioning. To cope with the high loads, a HEM 280 section was required for the upper chord, a HEB 300 for the lower one. Owing to their flange and web thicknesses, the sections selected have very different load-carrying capacities, even though their overall dimensions are very similar – which gives the finished lattice beam a very balanced appearance. The vertical struts of the lattice beam are formed from HEB or HEA 160 sections depending on the loading case and are

7   Valeo motors plant, Beitigheim-Bissingen, 2003
    Architects: Ackermann & Partner
    Structural engineer: Christoph Ackermann
8   View of roof as "fifth facade" with external lattice
    beams and self-supporting northlights for admit-
    ting daylight. This non-glare lighting arrangement
    is a reliable way of creating an optimum work-
    place quality and also improves the building's
    energy balance.
9   Longitudinal section, scale 1:250
10 Section through lattice beam showing suspended
    secondary beams, scale 1:250
11 Detail of lattice beam with solid round section
    diagonals welded to gusset plates, scale 1:20
12 Section through lattice beam showing connection
    of secondary beam hangers, scale 1:20

8

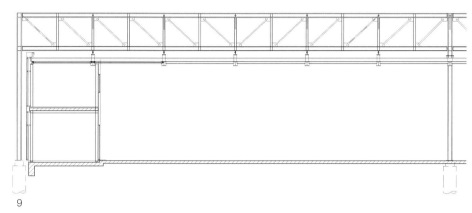

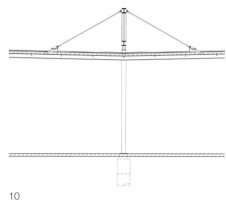

9

10

welded rigidly to the top and bottom chords, which are in turn additionally stiffened at each of these connections. The diagonal ties are made from solid round bars connected to welded gusset plates – necessary to achieve the length of weld seam required. The cross-sectional area of the ties is increased to handle higher tensile stresses at certain points.

The assembly at the nodes of the lattice beam must ensure that the system lines of the sections and diagonals all coincide at one point in order to guarantee a clean transfer of the forces. Lattice beams with open rolled sections and welded ties, like the one shown here, can be produced very economically.

The system of secondary beams is positioned within the building envelope and is supported on diagonal ties attached to the top chords of the lattice beams plus vertical plates beneath the bottom chords. Forked-end eye-bars were used because these are simple to erect on site. They can be easily attached to the plates welded to the top chords and subsequently adjusted.

The connection between these diagonal hangers and the secondary beams is by way of plates above the waterproofing, which considerably simplified the sealing at the penetration. Generally speaking, penetrating the roof requires great care, especially with regard to the waterproofing.

Corrosion protection is a very important issue for external loadbearing structures. On this project, hot-dip galvanising plus primer and finish coats represents the best possible protection. However, when the parts are too large, galvanising is often impossible and therefore the make-up of the corrosion protection must be very carefully considered (see pages 79–83).

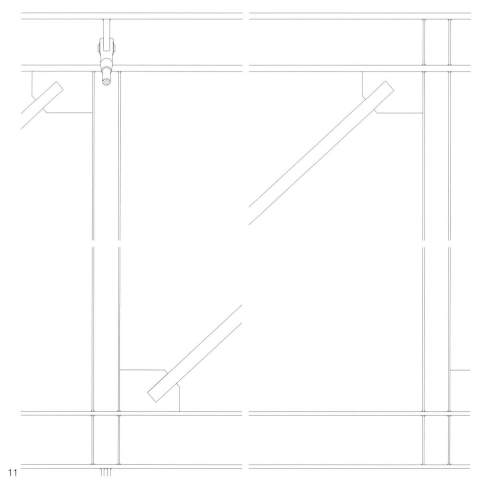

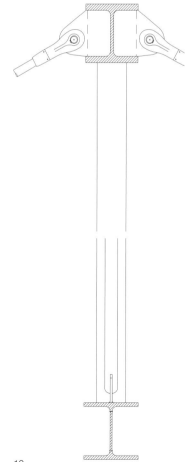

11

12

13

Lattice beams as primary and secondary beams in one plane

The original idea for this loadbearing concept was a non-directional beam system that can be extended as required in any direction while also achieving the necessary spans without intervening columns disrupting the production. In order to optimise the structural design, the drawings for the building services and production plant were taken into account during the concept phase. Many revision stages finally led to a 24.5 m square grid with main beams continuous in the longitudinal direction of the shed supporting single-span secondary beams. Both main and secondary elements consist of lattice beams at the same level to optimise the installation of services.

The sections for the lattice beams were rigorously chosen to match the respective loads: members subjected purely to tension are made from steel flats, ties with minor compression loads are made from narrow channels, and struts at risk of buckling are made from doubly symmetric rolled sections. This not only saves material, but makes the functions of the various parts very obvious.

Diagonals made from solid round bars connected with turnbuckles form a plate at roof level which transfers the wind loads to the concrete cores or vertical bracing. In addition, the roof-level ties provide lateral restraint to the upper chords of the lattice beams, which are at risk of buckling. The vertical girders bracing the entire construction are in the plane of the facade in the middle of this 171.5 m long shed; the loadbearing structure can thus expand without restraint in both directions. This halves the maximum possible displacement.

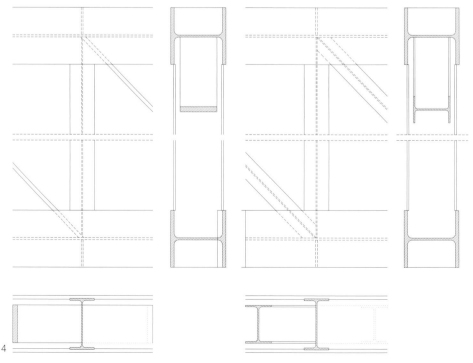

13 Valeo wipers plant, Beitigheim-Bissingen, 2002
    Architects: Ackermann & Partner
    Structural engineer: Christoph Ackermann
14 The individual sections of the lattice beam are
    tailored to suit the respective loads, scale 1:20   14

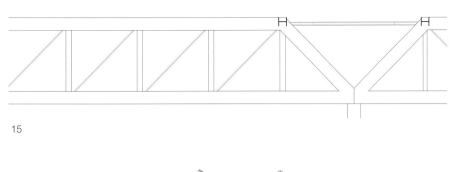

15

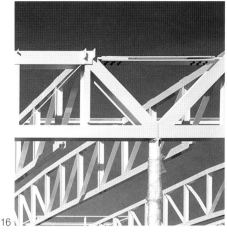

16

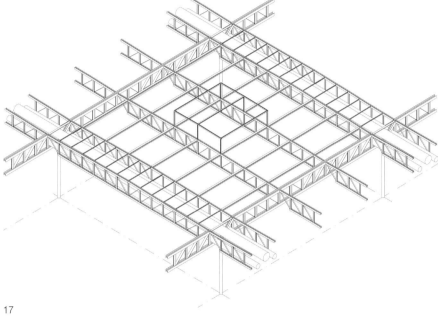

17

15 Elevation on main beam
16 The 24.5 m long main beam segments are spliced
    at each support. In order to accommodate the
    high moments in these continuous beams at this
    point, the top chord slopes down to the bottom
    chord and at the top the gap is bridged by a flat
    steel tie, which is easy to fix on site. The second-
    ary beams hung between the main beams must
    be offset from the line of the columns, but this
    does create a large space for building services.
17 Isometric view of one structural module with
    rooftop lantern
18 Column-beam connection showing erection
    splice between continuous main beams,
    scale 1:20

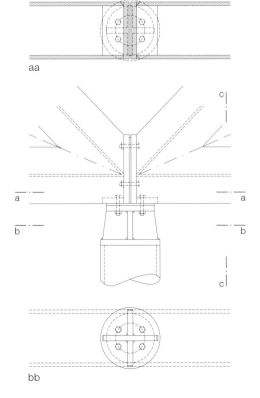

aa

a   a

b   b

c   c

18   bb

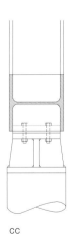

cc

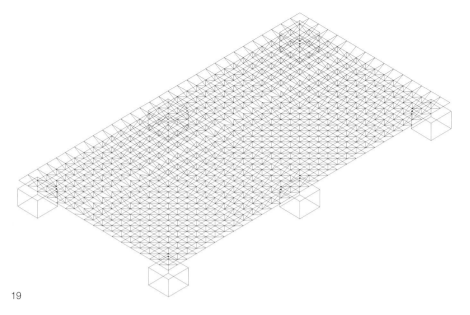

19

Welded beam grid with special castings at the joints

The floor area of this single-storey shed measures 27 400 m². The building is 226.26 m long, 121.26 m wide and 18.60 m high.

The primary structure consists of a beam grid resolved into steel lattice beams in both directions with an overall depth of 4.50 m. This grid is supported on six reinforced concrete service cores, which ensure the necessary stability for the whole building. The 7.50 m square grid is the result of a constructional and economic optimisation process based on the circular hollow sections used. The secondary structure consists of prefabricated timber sandwich panels measuring 2.50 x 7.50 m, which are laid chessboard fashion on supports mounted on the grid.

A combination of linear and point supports was chosen for the primary structure. The load is supported at eight points (max. support reaction: 1100 tonnes) on the inner corners of the service cores constructed from in situ reinforced concrete. This combination results in a fixity effect at the corner and middle cores for resisting the wind loads (fig. 21).

The primary structure consists of hot-worked circular hollow sections (grade St 355 JO, formerly St 52-U) which are connected rigidly by welding to special castings at the nodes. The top chords are loaded primarily in compression in the spans, but primarily in tension at the fixed supports above the service cores. The bottom chords are in tension in the spans and in compression over the supports. The diameters and wall thicknesses of the sections were adapted to suit the particular loads. The diagonals are subjected to

both tension and compression in the vicinity of the fixed supports. Over the supports they are therefore in the form of X-bracing in order to distribute the loads in tension and compression. In doing so, the ties support the struts and thus reduce their effective length for buckling. The loadbearing members are joined rigidly together at the system nodes via special castings in GS 18 NiMo Cv 3Y6 material. The advantage of the method of casting – part-moulds are combined to form complete moulds – was used to develop a modular system for the joints. Using main sections and various attachments, any type of connection arrangement involving diagonals and posts could be manufactured. The rigid primary structure has a camber of 500 mm. Under maximum loading (dead loads plus snow load), the vertical deformation can reach 300 mm, but the remaining camber of about 200 mm prevents an "apparent" sagging of the construction. The primary structure was prefabricated in 30 m long segments at the works which were then erected and welded together on site.

20

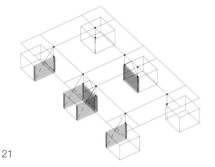

21

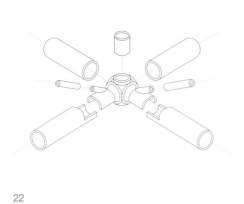

22

23

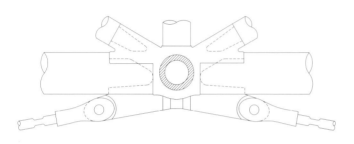

24

19 Sketch of roof structure system showing the
    eight support points
20 Hall 13 built for EXPO 2000, Hannover, 1997
    Architects: Ackermann & Partner
    Structural engineers: Schlaich, Bergermann &
    Partner
21 Sketch showing bracing concept
22 Isometric view of cast node to which the circular
    hollow sections are welded
23 Lattice-beam grid with roof covering of timber
    sandwich panels
24 Connection of longitudinal bracing to cast node
    in the vicinity of the central core, not to scale
25, 26 Support point with transverse bracing

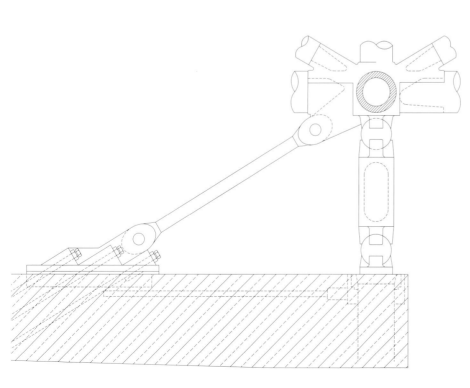

25

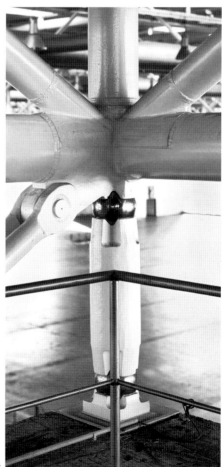

26

Semi-finished products of steel

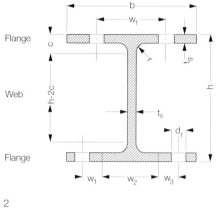

1 Blooming train, Salzgitter AG, hot-rolling process for an I-section
2 Wide I-section with parallel flanges, HEB series = IPB to DIN 1025-2

Steel is a hot- and cold-workable alloy of iron with a carbon content < 1.9%. The commercial semi-finished products formed by rolling, extruding or drawing are covered by standards. Hot-working methods include
- hot rolling,
- forging
- casting
- extruding

Hot-working takes place above the so-called recrystallisation temperature, cold-working below this temperature. The cold-working methods include:

- drawing   (prestressing wires)
- deep drawing   (sheets for trapezoidal profiles)
- cold twisting   (reinforcing bars)
- cold bending   (prestressing bars)
- cold heading   (heads on prestressing wires)
- cold rolling   (sections)

The overall term semi-finished product stands for prefabricated raw materials that are ready for further processing, e.g. sheets, sections or pipes. These semi-finished materials represent the usual forms supplied to the metalworking industry. They are not made-to-order elements representing rational and cost-effective constructions. They are mass-produced prefabricated goods that require only specific further processing or finishing. Steel products are described in EN 10079 according to form, dimensions, appearance and surface finish. We make a basic distinction between the following:

- Sections, bars and wires
  Hot-rolled sections, hollow sections (seamless and welded pipes), cold-formed sections, wires (rolled, drawn)
- Plates and sheets
  Wide flats, sheets and strips (hot- or cold-rolled), profiled sheets

Sections, bars and wires
Ingot casting involves casting the molten steel from the converters in moulds (chills) to form slabs or blooms.
A newer method is continuous casting in which blanks with the desired length are formed:

- blooms > 130 mm^2
- billets < 130 mm^2
- slabs $t > 40$ mm
- hot- and cold-rolled strips

The various steel sections are then manufactured from these products in hot-rolling mills, where the red-hot blooms or slabs pass through several mill stands until the section has reached its final shape and dimensions. Section products are supplied straight, rolled wires in coils. More than 70 000 different rolled steel products can be produced. The most common standard rolled sections are listed in tables together with their cross-sectional properties and geometries in European and DIN standards plus the works standards of the foundries. Custom sections are also possible, but are only economic when ordered in large quantities. In Germany, the standardised European sections are the most common sections employed. However, sections for exporting overseas, and defined according to international standards, are also available. Tables giving the surface area in m^2/m for the various sections simplify the calculation of areas for rust removal and painting work. The section development figure U in m^2 is used to determine the section factor U/A for fire protection requirements. The smaller the U/A ratio, the thinner the cladding can be for a given fire resistance class.
Steel prices are based on weight. The

weight figures can also be found in the tables of the various sections and other products, and those weights form the basis for the price calculation. The weights are based on a density of 7.85 kg/dm^3 as specified by the Iron & Steel Committee (DIN 18335 and DIN 18360).
Economic design and construction are only possible with corresponding knowledge and experience. In some forms of construction it can be more economic to use the high-grade S355 (formerly St 52) steel than the cheaper S235 (formerly St 37). Different sections carry different price tags and so the lightest section is not always the cheapest. When selecting sections, the processing in the works and erection on site must be taken into consideration as well as the structural requirements and price.

I-sections
The most frequent section met with in practice is the I-section. An I-section is formed by passing the semi-finished product through a series of pairs of rolls. A characteristic feature of this form of rolling is the radiused corners between web and flanges. The sections are rolled in one direction, which results in the principal strength lying in the rolling direction; the transverse strength is lower. Sections produced in this way have a high dimensional accuracy, but the production process does have its limits. The permissible tolerances are specified in the standards and must be taken into account during planning and design work. One outcome of this is that all stiffeners fitted between the flanges of I-sections must be produced individually for each case and cannot be stocked as standard products. In the range of European I-sections, the section designation is identical with the depth of the section for the HEB (standard series) and IPE sections (continued on page 68).

3a   b   c

Overview of customary European standardised steel sections – forms and applications, dimensions and weights

Designation	min./max. dimensions (h x b) [mm]		Weight [kg/m]	DIN standard	Euronorm EN
Sections with parallel flanges					
• IPE	IPE 80	(80 × 46 mm)	6.0 kg/m	DIN 1025-5	EN 19–57/44–63
medium-wide I-beam	IPE 600	(600 × 220 mm)	122.0 kg/m		
• IPET	IPET 80	(40 × 46 mm)	3.0 kg/m		
halved IPE	IPET 600	(300 × 220 mm)	61.2 kg/m	DIN EN 59051 (sharp-edged sections)	
• UPE	UPE 80	(80 × 50 mm)	7.9 kg/m	DIN 1026-2 (Peiner Träger GmbH)	
channel	UPE 400	(400 × 115 mm)	72.2 kg/m		
• UAP	UAP 60 × 45	(60 × 45 mm)	8.4 kg/m	French standard NFA 45-255 (Arbed)	
channel	UAP 300 × 100	(300 mm × 100 mm)	46.0 kg/m		

IPE   UAP   IPET

IPE sections are slender, lighter sections for low loads. Owing to the limited flange width, there is a risk of buckling, and IPEs are therefore chiefly used as beams – are less suitable as struts or columns. Frequently used in multi-storey construction. UPE and UAP sections are often used in pairs; used singly as a beam, the asymmetric form permits only low loads because it tends to rotate under load.
IPET beams are non-standardised IPE beams halved by fabricators; used as chords in lattice beams or as beams in composite floor constructions where the floor is supported on the bottom flange.

Wide-flange beams

Designation	min./max. dimensions (h x b) [mm]		Weight [kg/m]	DIN standard	Euronorm EN
• HEA light series (IPBl)	HEA 100	(96 × 100 mm)	16.7 kg/m	DIN 1025-3	EN 53–62/34–62
wide I-beam, light series	HEA 1000	(990 × 300 mm)	272.0 kg/m		
• HEB standard series (IPB)	HEB 100	(100 × 100 mm)	20.4 kg/m	DIN 1025-2	EN 53–62/34–62
wide I-beam, standard series	HEA 1000	(1000 × 300 mm)	314.0 kg/m		
• HEM heavy series (IPBv)	HEM 100	(120 × 106 mm)	41.8 kg/m	DIN 1025-4	EN 53–62/34–62
wide I-beam, heavy series	HEM 1000	(1008 × 302 mm)	349.0 kg/m		

HEA   HEB   HEM

For high loads (columns, beams), parallel flanges, radiused corners.
High buckling stability owing to wide flange and therefore also suitable for transverse loads.
Compact, square cross-section.
Caution: The profile designation only matches the actual section depth in the case of the HEB series, e.g. HEB 200.
In the HEB series depth and width are identical for the 100–300 mm sections; above this the width remains constant at 300 mm.
The same applies to the HEA and HEM series.

Standard sections (tapered flanges)

Designation	min./max. dimensions (h x b) [mm]		Weight [kg/m]	DIN standard	Euronorm EN
• INP	INP 80	(80 × 42 mm)	5.9 kg/m	DIN 1025, sht 1	
narrow I-beam	INP 500	(500 × 185 mm)	141.0 kg/m		
• UNP	UNP 80	(80 × 45 mm)	8.6 kg/m	DIN 1026	EN 24–62
U-Stahl	UNP 400	(400 × 110 mm)	71.8 kg/m		

INP   UNP

Owing to the tapered internal flange surfaces, these sections are seldom used for bolted constructions, but tend to be welded.
Can be used for secondary components, e.g. purlins.
Standard sections are less expensive than sections with parallel flanges, but are still only rarely used these days.

British universal beams (UB) and universal columns (UC)

Designation	min./max. dimensions (h x b) [mm]		Weight [kg/m]	DIN standard	Euronorm EN
• UB	UB 127 × 76 × 13	(127 mm × 76 mm)	13 kg/m		
	UB 914 × 419 × 388	(921 mm × 420 mm)	388 kg/m		
• UC	UC 152 × 152 × 23	(152 mm × 152 mm)	23 kg/m		
	UC 356 × 406 × 634	(474 mm × 424 mm)	634 kg/m		

UB   UC

Dimensions and properties to BS 4: Part 1:1993

For other sections according to international standards see p. 106

d   e   f

Overview of customary European standardised steel sections – forms and applications, dimensions and weights

Designation	min./max. dimensions (h x b) [mm]		Weight [kg/m][1]	DIN standard	Euronorm EN
Hollow sections	**(Wall thicknesses vary)**				
RRW/RRK square	RRW 40 × 40	(40 × 40 mm)	4.4 kg/m		
	RRW 400 × 400	(400 × 400 mm)	191.0 kg/m	Hot-worked, DIN EN 10210	
RRW/RRK rectangular	RRW 50 × 30	(50 × 30 mm)	4.4 kg/m		
	RRW 400 × 200	(400 × 200 mm)	141.0 kg/m	Cold-worked, DIN EN 10219	
ROR circular	ROR 38	(38 mm)	2.0 kg/m		
	ROR 600	(600 mm)	114.0 kg/m		

[1] Weight depends on wall thickness
The external dimensions can be maintained but the wall thickness varied to cope with different loads.
From the structural viewpoint, circular hollow sections have an optimum column cross-section, a small surface development (favourable U/A value, less painting required). Ideal for concentric loads on columns and for lattice beams. Often used for exposed forms of construction. We distinguish between RRK (cold-worked), lightweight and inexpensive, and RRW (hot-worked), with good buckling resistance due to upset corners.

square   rectangular   circular

Bars[2]					
RND (round section)	RND 5.5	(Ø 5,5 mm)	0.2 kg/m	DIN 1013	EN 60
	RND 400	(Ø 400 mm)	986.4 kg/m		
VKT (square section)	VKT 6	(6 × 6 mm)	0.3 kg/m	DIN 1014	EN 59
	VKT 200	(200 × 200 mm)	314.0 kg/m		
FL (flat)	5 × 10	(5 × 10 mm)	0.4 kg/m	DIN 1017 pt 1 & 2	EN 58–78
	60 × 150	(60 × 150 mm)	70.7 kg/m	DIN EN 10058	

max. 150 mm

[2] Hexagonal and custom sections are also classed as bars.
Solid bars are very uneconomic as struts, but they can achieve a high fire resistance class when used in conjunction with a suitable fire protection system. Solid bars are primarily used as ties. The narrow flat saves space, but the ends must be widened or thickened with additional plates to compensate for weakening due to holes. When provided with a thread at each end, round bars can be lengthened by joining with screwed sleeves.

Angle and small sections

Common sections for general metalworking requirements (balustrades, canopies, simple doors and windows, etc.)

1	Equal angle – radiused corners	7	Equal angle – sharp corners	13	Equal angle – cold-rolled
2	Unequal angle – radiused corners	8	Unequal angle – sharp corners	14	Unequal angle – cold-rolled
3	T-section – radiused corners, long stalk	9	T-section – sharp corners	15	Plain channel – cold-rolled
4	Channel	10	Plain channel	16	Z-section – cold-rolled
5	Z-section – standard section	11	Z-section – sharp corners	17	Outwardly lipped channel – cold-rolled
6	Flat	12	Balustrade tube	18	Inwardly lipped channel – cold-rolled

```
L    L    ⊥    ⊔    ⌐    ─
1    2    3    4    5    6

L    L    ⊥    ⊔    ⌐    O
7    8    9    10   11   12

L    L         ⊔    ⌐    ⊔    ⊏
13   14        15   16   17   18
```

Angle and small sections (see above)

3   a–h The diversity of steel sections held in stock,
    Donges Stahlbau

g   h

The HEA (light form) and HEM (heavy form) sections differ only in terms of their flange and web thicknesses. The internal dimensions are identical because only one pair of web rolls in the mill train is replaced during production.

The shape of a rolled steel section is optimised to suit the way it primarily carries loads. The classic I-section, in structural terms a beam in bending, has strong top and bottom flanges in the compression and tension zones, joined by a narrow web. This is an efficient cross-sectional form because each part of the section is designed to fulfil a specific function. The flanges carry normal (axial) stresses caused by bending moments while the web carries the shear forces.

The material technologies specific to steel such as rolling, shaping and welding enable an optimum cross-sectional shape to be achieved that can be matched to the respective loadbearing behaviour. This results in an economic use of the material.

U-Profile

The asymmetric position of the shear centre is the reason why single channels are seldom used in practice as primary structural elements. Bending about the strong axis almost always results in rotation of the section. Closed, thin-wall hollow sections are more suitable for torsional-buckling loads than open ones (channels or I-sections).

However, channels act like I-sections when coupled together in pairs to overcome the rotation problem. Great attention must be paid to preventing corrosion in the unavoidable gap between the backs of the channels (see DIN EN ISO 12944-3).

Hollow sections

Rolled steel hollow sections may have square, rectangular or circular cross-sections. There are two forms depending on the type of manufacture:

- The welded, seamless pipe that is drawn over a mandrel and rolled flat.
- The welded pipe with a visible seam – made from a sheet formed into a hollow section and then the edges joined with a longitudinal or spiral weld.

Circular pipes are usually the starting point for all other hollow section geometries because such pipes are simply subsequently hot- or cold-worked accordingly. They must be protected against internal corrosion (pitting). Hollow sections are approx. 1.5 to 2 times more expensive than rolled sections ex works and the connection details are more complicated than with open sections.

Flats

According to DIN EN 10058, steel flats belong to the section and bar products and not to the plate and sheet products. They are produced in widths between 10 and 150 mm, and therefore they do indeed appear more like bars than plates. Their weight is specified in kg/m. Lengths up to 13 m are possible.

Drawn steel

Drawn steel is produced through the hot- or cold-drawing of rolled wires. Rolled wires are semi-finished products which are randomly stacked in coils while still hot. The thickness is usually > 5 mm and the surface finish is smooth, but the cross-section varies. Drawing gradually reduces the cross-section. Drawn steel is employed for very long steel products (wire, reinforcing bars). Hot-rolled bars are supplied as straight bars, not in coils.

Plates and sheets

These steel products include:
- heavy and medium plates
- light plates
- cold-formed sections
- perforated plates
- profiled sheets

Thicker flat metal products are known as plates, the thinner ones as sheets. Slabs form the raw material; they are passed through various mill stands to reduce them to the required thickness. The thinner the final product, the higher is the number of passes required. Sheets and plates are rolled in two directions and therefore they can carry loads in both directions. That makes them suitable for gusset plates, for instance. Sheets and plates are supplied flat in widths from 1000 to 1600 mm.

On the other hand, a strip is a sheet product that is rolled into a coil (max. 1250 mm wide) directly after rolling. Without further processing, the smooth strip of the unrolled coil tends to suffer from warping due to internal stresses and when under load. Folding is one way of making sheets stiffer in the direction of the folds.

4   IPE beam section notched ready for a beam-beam connection, with web predrilled and first coat of primer already applied.
5   Heavy plates of various thicknesses
    Laser cutting techniques enable any shapes to be produced.
6   Hollow sections

7

8

9

Heavy plates

Heavy and medium plates are steel products identified by thickness (t), width (b) and length. Any form of building components can be produced from this flat material through hot- or cold-working and welding. Malleability and suitability for welding are the quality features here. Heavy plates with thicknesses of 8–250 mm are used for steel buildings and bridges. Indeed, for spans exceeding 150 m, welded plate constructions are the most popular solution. Welded sections can be custom-fabricated from individual plates and/or standard beams to suit particular requirements and designs. Flanges and webs or box sections are welded together from individual plates. However, owing to the extra work required, welded sections are more expensive than standard rolled sections.

Heavy plates in thicknesses of 5–80 mm and widths of 150–1250 mm are also treated like wide steel flats. Their exact dimensions in mm and weights in kg/m can be found in the section tables of the manufacturers.

Plates with rolled patterns (chequer, lozenge, studded, etc., see DIN 59220) and non-slip surface finishes are also among the plate and sheet products available. DIN 51130/ZHI/571 provides details of non-slip finishes.

The range of steel grades for heavy plates extends from unalloyed steel to high-alloy austenitic steels. For example, fire-resistant mild steel FR30, which is a special alloy which undergoes special rolling, is also available in heavy plate form (thicknesses from 5 to 50 mm) for the fabrication of welded sections.

Light plates

Light plates are fabricated in cold-rolling mills. The plates are produced in continuous strip casting and rolled out to the desired thickness. The plate is given a colour coating and/or galvanised finish in several passes direct from the coil, and cold-worked afterwards. The most common methods of processing (see DIN 8580) are:

- Re-forming through deep drawing (pressing, upsetting, bending, curving, folding, profiling, flanging)
- Cutting to size (punching, sawing, laser cutting)
- Surface treatments (brushing, pickling, polishing, shot-blasting, painting, powder coating, electrogalvanising, hot-dip galvanising, enamelling, anodising, laminating)

Cold-formed sections

These sections are produced through the further processing of finished plates or sheets, or from hot- or cold-rolled coils or from wide steel flats. Cold-forming, at room temperature, changes the micro-structure of the steel. The dislocation density increases and the yield stress rises, but the ductility decreases. Therefore, high-strength wires are also cold-drawn. In doing so, the steel must exhibit certain values for tensile strength and elongation at rupture. The rolling of cold-worked sheets and plates results in an increase in strength at the bending points, but at the same time a tendency towards embrittlement. Frequent bending back and forth leads to destruction of the crystalline structure. Characteristic of such sections is their almost constant material thickness throughout the section. Thin-wall sections are rolled, but thicker webs and flanges are folded step by step (for smaller quantities) or cold-rolled (for larger quantities). We distinguish between three methods of manufacture: drawing, folding and profile rolling (series production). The cross-sections are not standardised. Building authority approvals are available for some sections of certain manufacturers. Only such sections can be used because they are not designed according to DIN 18800 like steel. Cold-worked steels – unlike hot-rolled sections – provide the chance of a cost-effective intervention in the production process for the creation of custom sections. Cross-sectional forms and dimensions can therefore be optimised and adapted for particular purposes, and

Flat-rolled products (plates, sheets, strips)

Type	Thickness [mm]	DIN standard	Properties
Heavy plate	> 4.75 mm	DIN 1543	floor plates, 3–20 mm
Medium plate	3.00–4.75 mm	DIN 1542	
Light plate	0.35–3.00 mm	DIN 1541	untreated = black plate with improved surface finish = coil-coated (e.g. aluminising, hot-dip galvanising, hot-dip galvanising + plastic coating)
Cold-formed sections	Sections made from flat-rolled steel with almost identical wall thickness. Formed by rolling (0.4–8.0 mm thick) and folding (up to 20 mm thick). DIN 59413, DASt-Ri 016 plus works standards. Many different shapes and dimensions.		
Profiled sheets	Corrugated and trapezoidal profiles; made from roll-profiled light plates with a high load-carrying capacity. 500–1050 mm wide, 10–200 mm deep, 0.65–1.50 mm material thickness, sheet lengths up to 22 m. (Ref: Stahlbau-Arbeitshilfe 44 & 44.2, DIN 18807 parts 1-3, June 1987 ed.)		

10

7 Hot-rolled plates of various thicknesses marked to enable easy identification in the stockyard
8 Typical flooring plate products with folded/bent edges, galvanised
9 Galvanised light plates stand ready for further processing
10 Forms of supply for rolled products for use in structural steelwork

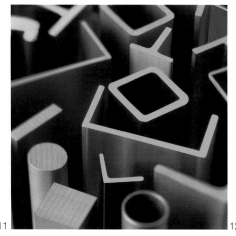

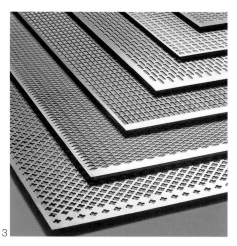

11   12   13

this is why such sections are often fabricated to order for specific projects. Despite the diversity of cold-formed sections, there is a series of customary standard sections that are also available at short notice, e.g. I-sections, angles, channels, Z-sections, inwardly and outwardly lipped channels, Σ-sections and Ω-sections, plus slit circular, square and rectangular sections. Sections are classified according to their cross-sectional form:

- open – closed
- symmetrical – asymmetrical
- orthogonal – non-orthogonal

Cold-formed sections with thin material thicknesses are difficult to connect. The cold-forming process makes the material unsuitable for welding and the thin webs and flanges mean that the bolting and screwing options are also restricted.

Perforated plates and sheets
DIN 4185-2 and DIN 24041 specify sheets and plates with identical openings at regular spacings produced by way of punching, perforating or drilling. All grades of steel, even corrosion-resistant, heat-resistant and hardwearing steels,

can be perforated, in thicknesses from 0.5 mm (black plate) to 30 mm (heavy plate). The perforations are produced on presses or with automatic punching machines, either in large series direct from the coil or from individual sheets/plates:

- Small format   1000 mm × 2000 mm
- Medium format 1250 mm × 2500 mm
- Large format   1500 mm × 3000 mm
- Super format   1600 mm × 4000 mm
- Coil   widths up to 1250 mm
                         max. 2 mm thick

Inquiries or orders must state whether sheet/plates with or without unperforated edges are required. With an unperforated edge, the dimensions of the end and side strips must be specified. When manufactured from coils and cut to size afterwards, the cuts pass through the perforations across the width, but there is always a narrow unperforated strip along both longitudinal edges. Perforated sheets and plates fabricated from ready-cut stock materials can be provided with perforations right up to the edges on all sides if required.

The perforations, just as much as the thickness of the material, influence the properties of the product. High stiffness and unrestricted throughflow require circular holes offset by 60°, which is the most common form of perforation (standard form). Contrasting with this, plates and sheets with straight rows of circular openings exhibit a lower stiffness (decorative perforations for shutters, furniture, etc.). An important point is that the size of the hole should not be less than the thickness of the material. Like every light plate, perforated plates can also be further processed using all manner of techniques. This versatile, simple handling and the ensuing high degree of factory prefabrication results in an inexpensive building product. The perforations reduce the weight of the building component – an economic advantage in lightweight construction. Perforated plates are also ideal as backing elements to sound-attenuating panels. Perforated plates can be used as loadbearing elements when folded to form treads and platforms, or laid as walkways on uncompacted ground. Additional indentations and ribs make them suitable for use as non-slip stair treads or floor coverings in industrial situations.

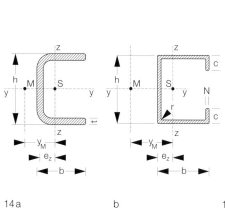

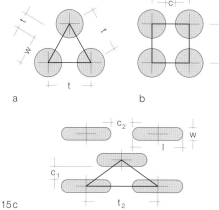

14 a   b   15 c

Abbreviations for dimensioning types of perforation using the examples of:
a round holes in offset rows
b round holes in straight rows
c elongated holes in offset rows

Important information for ordering perforated products:
- *Hole form f*
  Round holes (R) straight or offset, square holes (Q), elongated holes (L, Le) longitudinal and transverse, diamond and decorative holes
- *Hole dimensions*
  Hole width w (the minimum dimension for the perforation), hole length l (for rectangular geometry)
- *Hole spacing*
  Hole pitch t (centre-to-centre spacing of holes), web width c (minimum unperforated intermediate space)

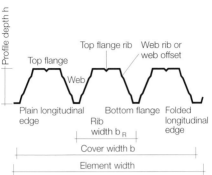

16

17

18

Profiled sheets

Profiled sheets are fabricated from light plates 0.65–1.50 mm thick. Specific folding and bending of this thin material creates webs and ribs that considerably increase the stability in the longitudinal direction, thus reducing the risk of buckling. The high load-carrying capacity of these extremely lightweight cold-worked sheet steel products makes them an indispensable element in lightweight construction. Profiled sheets can therefore be laid directly on the primary beams without the need for any secondary beams. Various semi-finished products made from light plates, also systems comprising corrugated, trapezoidal and pan profiles plus sandwich panels, are available for the roof, suspended floor and wall constructions of structural steelwork projects. They are supplied in the form of lightweight, large-format elements, usually made from galvanised and coated sheet steel with smooth or profiled surfaces. They are quick and easy to erect and their surfaces require no further treatment. The choice of profile depends on the structural requirements, which in turn depend on the spacing of the supporting members and the desired appearance. Changes in length due to thermal effects and wind suction forces govern the size and number of fixings required. Sliding connections and expansion joints at appropriate intervals can help prevent restraint stresses and overstressing of the material. Increased wind suction peaks occur at corners and edges (see DIN 1055-4) and suitable fixing arrangements must be allowed for at such places. Lightweight construction often makes use of multi-leaf thermally insulated wall assemblies made from profiled sheets. The thermal bridges that ensue due to this form of construction can be minimised by the use of insulating strips placed between the inner leaf and the spacer sections.

Corrugated sheets

The first roof coverings of corrugated sheet appeared in 1830. Corrugated sheet is loadbearing in one direction only; it can be rolled up in the other! Corrugated sheets are used primarily as weather protection in the case of simple structures. When used as the outer layer of a multi-layer roof or wall construction with an air cavity, a trapezoidal profile sheet is usually used as the loadbearing layer. Only limited depths are possible with corrugated sheets, and so the load-carrying capacity is restricted. Corrugated sheets can be supplied in lengths up to 14 m, which enables transverse joints to be avoided on many roofs. However, the recommended roof pitches must be taken into account, which depends on the particular profile.

Trapezoidal profile sheets

Steel trapezoidal profile sheets have been used in construction projects since 1950. They are formed in a continuous process from coils of galvanised steel supplied in thicknesses of 0.65-1.50 mm. This usually produces a cross-section with a trapezium-type shape, which means they can be loaded in one direction only. DIN 18807 regulates their dimensions and use. Thin-wall building components tend to exhibit severe deformations, especially transverse to the loadbearing direction. Their load-carrying capacity depends on maintaining the cross-sectional geometry – flattening tends to disrupt the loadbearing behaviour because the structural depth is reduced. The geometry of these profiles is therefore the subject of ongoing optimisation and the bending stiffness is always being improved by the addition of ribs and further profiling in the flange and web portions. These developments can be broken down into trapezoidal profiles of the first, second and third generations. Profiles of the first generation,

approx. 50 mm deep, were used exclusively as non-loadbearing cladding. Profiles of the second generation, with ribs and depths of 40–160 mm, are able to carry loads (rib spacing approx. 250 mm). These are available in lengths of up to 12 m (even up to 22 m if transport allows!) and so are ideal for use as continuous floors or roofs spanning over two or three bays (spans of 7.5–9.0 m are possible). The third generation is characterised by ribs on the top flange in the transverse direction and depths of up to 210 mm. Every manufacturer has developed his own profile geometries, each of which requires its own rollformer. This is why the trapezoidal profiles available are so diverse and the profiling has not been standardised. Every manufacturer therefore supplies his own design tables – including maximum spans in terms of profile depth, rib spacing and material thickness – based on building authority approvals.

11 Cold-formed sections
12 Coils of light plate with improved surface finish (galvanised), ready for further processing.
13 Perforated plates with various perforations
14 a Cold-formed section made from flat-rolled steel sheet, with thick walls, cold-formed by rolling or folding.
    b Inwardly lipped channel section made from light plate, with thin walls, almost no radii at the corners, used for lightweight steelwork construction.
15 Abbreviations for dimensioning types of perforation
16 Profiled sheets of the third generation
    Suspended floor profile with high bending stiffness due to two ribs in the top flange and deep profile geometry. Spans (with concrete topping) up to 5.50 m are feasible – useful for reducing the number of columns in multi-storey car parks and multi-storey buildings.
17 Designations for trapezoidal profiled sheets to DIN 18807-1
18 Combination of trapezoidal profile sheets used as external cladding on curved and flat facades. Single-leaf perforated profiles can also be used as translucent facade elements, for shading or as spandrel panels.

19

20

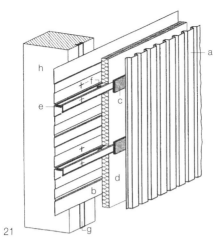

21

Steel trapezoidal profiles are used for suspended floors with or without a concrete topping. Trapezoidal profiles can therefore act as permanent formwork or contribute to the load-carrying capacity of a composite floor (see page 16). They can be used as the loadbearing layer and/or as the external weatherproof layer in roofs and walls. Roof constructions with two layers of trapezoidal profile sheets (at right-angles to each other) are also possible: the lower is the loadbearing layer upon which the thermal insulation is laid, which is separated from the upper layer (with a lower depth) by an air cavity which serves merely as protection against the weather. Trapezoidal profile sheets are protected against corrosion by means of hot-dip galvanising with or without an additional coating (DIN 18807-1). Fixing to supporting constructions, to each other or at the junctions with adjoining building components is by way of approved fasteners (self-drilling screws, shot-fired fixings, pop rivets – see information published by the IFBS, the German trade association for lightweight metal building systems). Welding, punching and lacing of the edges should be carried out only according to the manufacturer's specification. In the case of special acoustic requirements, profiles with perforated webs can be used to improve the sound attenuation.

Pans
These are produced through the cold-working of sheets with a thickness of 0.75-1.50 mm. Owing to their numerous ribs within the profile, they exhibit considerable stiffness. The elements are approx. 600 mm wide and 90-160 mm deep. Transport restrictions normally limit the maximum length to 12 m. Depending on the particular structural system, spans of up to 10 m are possible. They have narrow top flanges for fixing the outer leaf and a wide bottom flange with minimal profiling. Bottom flange plus webs form a compartment for thermal insulation. Joints between pans are sealed airtight with sealing tapes. Thermal breaks minimise the thermal bridges between the top flanges of the pan profiles and the outer leaf (fig. 21).
Pans achieve an optimised load-carrying capacity when used in conjunction with an outer leaf of steel trapezoidal profile sheets, but seldom when used together with corrugated sheets. The supporting framework and the outer leaf must then be carefully connected with approved fasteners at a close spacing to achieve a shear-resistant connection.
Generally, the outermost layer protects the construction against the weather and the building performance requirements are satisfied by the underlying layers. In

terms of function, we distinguish between forms of construction with and without an air cavity. In a wall with an air cavity, the external leaf is separated from the supporting construction by a layer of air. This prevents a build-up of condensation.

Sandwich panels
Sandwich panels are composite elements consisting of two thin, profiled sheet metal facings affixed to both sides of a core of mineral wool or rigid foam. The bond between facings and core must be shear-resistant. Such panels exhibit a high load-carrying capacity and, at the same time, good insulating properties, low weight and a low overall depth. They are also easy, quick and cost-effective to produce and install. Supplied as prefabricated elements, they can form the finished external envelope and the internal lining. The bending stiffness is determined solely by the sheet metal facings, the shear stiffness by the core. The surface profiling and colours of the coatings available are as diverse as the manufacture of the steel sheet itself.
On the building site, the panels are connected by way of preformed interlocking joints and attached to the supporting construction. Direct fixing from outside is possible with a self-tapping screw screwed through the panel and left

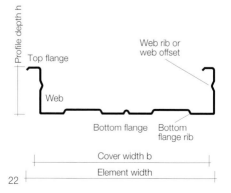

22

19 Facade cladding made from folded stainless steel panels
20 Sandwich panels with light steel plate facings
21 Construction of a thermally insulated pan wall
    a Outer leaf, trapezoidal profile sheet
    b Inner leaf, steel pan
    c Thermal break tape
    d Thermal insulation
    e Sealing strip between pans
    f Fastener
    g Steel cast-in channel
    h Column (reinforced concrete shown here)
22 Designations for steel pans to DIN 18807-1

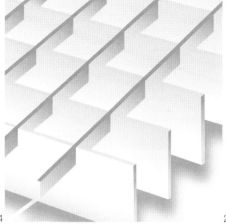

Material combinations and their composite functions

Type of material	Functions			
	Bond	Fire protect.	Sound insulation	Thermal insulation
Concrete	•	•	•	
Plasterboard	•	•	•	
Plywood	•		•	
Wood fibreboard	•		•	
Chipboard	○		•	
Mineral wool	○	•	•	•
Mineral fibres	○	•	•	•
Foam	○		○	•
Perlite	○	•	•	○

23   24   25

exposed. The indirect method of fixing employs screws in the joints, which means that the screw head is covered by the next panel. All fasteners must be easily removable for later maintenance work. As this form of construction has no air cavity, it is more vulnerable to any water or condensation that does infiltrate the construction. Joints and junctions must therefore be carefully considered during planning and properly executed on site. Draft European standard prEN 14509: 2004 specifies different types of joint. It is also important to coordinate the building grid according to openings in the wall and the dimensions of components in order to avoid unnecessary cutting and wastage. There is no standard for the design of sandwich elements; everything is regulated by building authority approvals – also the fasteners. Manufacturers publish tables of maximum spans to enable simplified design. Sandwich panels are incombustible when the thermal insulation complies with building materials class A2 to DIN 4102.

More and more building products with intelligent material combinations are now being developed under the heading of "composite". Such products can meet structural, thermal, sound and fire requirements simultaneously, and

include, for example, planar building elements made from sheet steel bonded to a core of mineral- or wood-based board materials. The aim is to achieve the building performance requirements but at the same time improve the loadbearing function of the sheet steel parts through their attachment to other, protective board materials. Building authority approval is required in every case.

Open-grid flooring, fabrics, meshes

Open-grid flooring

The construction principle of open-grid flooring depends on the alternation of bearing and transverse bars. The load is carried only by the bearing bars in the direction of those elements, with the span being measured between centres of support. The transverse bars are pressed into or welded to the bearing bars; they distribute the load and ensure stability. The perimeter frame surrounds the grid of bearing and transverse bars. Open-grid flooring is available in steel, stainless steel and aluminium.

When the transverse bars are pressed into shaped, punched notches in the bearing bars under high pressure, the result is a stable, non-twisting grid of

members, a so-called pressed grid (PR), which is chiefly used as open-grid flooring for foot traffic. To improve the non-slip effect of the flooring surface, both bearing and transverse bars can be serrated. Besides all the wide-mesh open-grid flooring types, it is particularly the close-mesh versions (mesh size 11 x 30, 30 x 11) that are suitable for foot traffic. The first dimension of the mesh size specifies the pitch of the bearing bars. Open-grid flooring for foot traffic usually has the longitudinal mesh parallel to the long side of the grid. Various fasteners and fittings (e.g. hook bolts, clips) are available to prevent break-ins, slippage or rattling of the grids. Hinges are available so that opening panels are also possible.

Welded pressed grids (SP) are produced by attaching twisted square steel bars in a combined welding and pressing process to the steel flat bearing bars (without notches for the transverse bars). Every intersection is welded, which results in a particularly homogeneous and twist-resistant grid. Such open-grid flooring not only has a higher load-carrying capacity than simple pressed grids, but also permits openings to be cut out.

When bearing and transverse bars are the same depth, this is known as a full grid (VR). The loadbearing effect of such grids is low and they can be used as

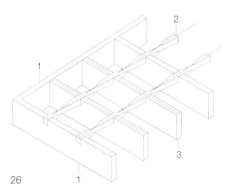

26

23   Various types of open-grid flooring, galvanised
24   Open-grid flooring with restricted view through
25   Combinations of materials and their functions in the composite construction
     • suitable
     ○ limited suitability
26   Welded and pressed open-grid flooring (schematic)
     1 Binding bar
     2 Transverse bar (twisted square bar)
     3 Bearing bar

27

28

29

balustrades, suspended ceilings or as sunshades. If the view through is to be restricted, the transverse bars can be placed at an angle, e.g. for bridges, walkways, ventilation grilles, balconies, sunshades and cladding. In this case the transverse bars are welded to the bearing bars at an angle of 30° or 45°. If this effect is desired with a full grid (VR), the bearing and transverse bars are simply pressed together, and therefore there is no limit to the angle of the transverse bars. The welding then no longer disturbs the visual appearance.

Expanded metal

The diamond-shaped openings of this semi-finished product are created by cutting offset slits in flat sheets or strips and then pulling the metal sideways. Nowadays, aperture sizes from 1.0 to 300 mm are possible. In contrast to perforated sheets and plates, no material is lost in the production process. Stretching the metal results in mesh-like openings that are neither woven nor welded. Expanded metal meshes can therefore be cut to any size without disturbing the overall coherence of the metal. The production process results in a twisting of the material, resulting in a three-dimensional, textured

appearance. However, if required, the finished product can be rolled flat up to a width of 1400 mm and a thickness of 3.0 mm.

Expanded metal is a product that is flat like perforated sheets but considerably less expensive. Thanks to its high stability, an open cross-section is possible, and transparent areas of 4–90% are feasible. In addition, it can be shaped and folded and has a low self-weight. This results in stable facade elements that place few demands on the supporting construction. As an inexpensive, stable alternative to wire fabrics, expanded metal is ideal for large facade elements, allowing good air circulation. The use of expanded metal as low-cost balustrade panels or for smaller gratings with low loads are also common applications. Screwed to angle frames or with bent-up edges, they can be used as folding partitions, movable light diffusers or privacy screens. Manufacturers of expanded metal can usually supply special steel sections for use as frames for expanded metal gratings and perforated panels.

When ordering expanded metal, the so-called long way and short way of the

mesh plus the strand width and material thickness must be specified, according to DIN 791. Note that the long way and short way figures indicate the distance between the centres of the so-called knuckles, not the clear opening size. Expanded metal is produced from sheet steel with a minimum elongation at rupture of 25%, also from stainless steel (e.g. material numbers 4301 and 4571) and non-ferrous metals (NE) such as copper, brass or aluminium.

Wire fabrics
Wire production
The method of producing wire by swaging through drawing dates from Celtic times. Steel suppliers can supply more than 250 different types of wire. With a carbon content below 0.25%, it is an iron wire product, but when the content is 0.25–1%, we speak of steel wire. Steel wire is as thin as a hair, is extremely resistant to breakage, and can be bent. Rolled wire is produced by the hot-rolling of billets cast in the steelworks. It is coiled up in a spiral behind the mill stand with a thickness of 5-55 mm (see fig. 29). After that, it is heat-treated (to harden it) and either given a surface finish treatment or

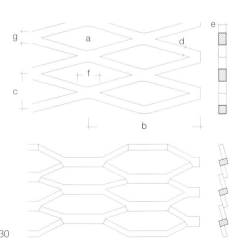

30

27 Expanded metal, with large open area
28 Expanded metal, aluminium
29 Red-hot wires being coiled up after rolling. After cooling, they are sent for further processing.
30 Two different examples of expanded metal (top: flattened; bottom: raised, i.e. conventional)
    a Aperture
    b Long way of mesh pitch
    c Nominal short way of mesh
    d Strand width
    e Thickness
    f Knuckle length
    g Knuckle width

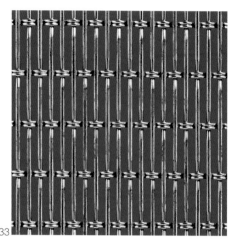

31

32

33

shaved, depending on the intended application. In the next step of the process, the material is drawn in wire and bar drawing works. For smaller diameters, the wire is drawn through one or more tapered dies in the drawing machine. Drawn wire has a thickness of 53–0.1 mm. This work is carried out by metalworking operations in drawing, wire rope, weaving and braiding shops, which produce strands, wire ropes and metal fabrics. Even screws, nuts and rivets can be produced from thicker, cold-headed wire.

Metal fabrics
A weaving process is employed to turn round or flat wires, wire ropes or strands (very fine wire ropes) into fabrics with standard widths on automatic mechanical looms. As with textiles, two intersecting thread systems are woven together at right-angles: the warp thread parallel to the length of the fabric and the weft thread transverse to it, which can be combined in different ways to create different weaves.
Weft threads are continuous, which creates a woven edge along both sides. As the warp threads are subject to higher mechanical loads during the weaving process, they are often thicker than the

weft threads. In contrast to braided and knitted fabrics, a woven fabric does not become narrower as the tensile load increases because the whole force is taken by the warp threads anyway. Depending on the wires chosen for the warp and weft threads plus the type of weave and surface finish, a whole variety of different mesh patterns is possible (for more information see DETAIL Practice "Translucent Materials", page 93). Again like textiles, woven metal fabrics have a right and a wrong side. But if the appearance of both sides is identical, we speak of a double-faced weave, e.g. plain weave. DIN ISO 4783 parts 1 and 3 plus DIN ISO 9044 regulates the marking of woven wire fabrics, wire meshes and screens. They provide a guide to the choice of combinations of mesh width and wire diameter. Woven wire fabrics are characterised by the type of weave (i.e. the way in which the warp and weft threads intersect) and the fineness of the weave (i.e. the number of stitches per inch). Further descriptive information is provided by the number of stitches (n) per cm^2, open screen area (A, F), mesh width (w), wire diameter (d) and fabric thickness (D). Woven wire fabrics are used for facades, cladding to multi-storey

car parks, as sound insulation and sun-shading elements, and as safety barriers. When used externally, the fabric must offer sufficient stability and resistance to environmental conditions. Depending on the angle of the incident light and the location, the material can appear either opaque or transparent.

The manufacturers of metal fabrics can supply a multitude of fixing and tensioning systems. Depending on the size of the elements, intermediate fixings may be necessary between the top and bottom fixings when hanging a fabric vertically. Square or round bars woven or inserted into the hem of the fabric are relatively easy to connect to the supporting construction. For external applications in

31 Warp wires being prepared for the weaving process to produce a woven metal fabric
32 Steel strands are produced by twisting the wires
33 Long-mesh fabric with pairs of stainless steel wires
34 Plain mesh with strands (warp) and bars (weft) in stainless steel
35 Round-wire braided element, bright or galvanised steel, also available with flat wires
36 Round-wire belt in widths up to 3000 mm, bright or galvanised steel, also available with flat wires

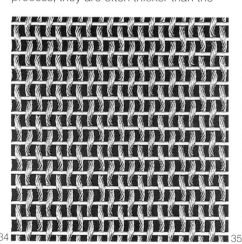
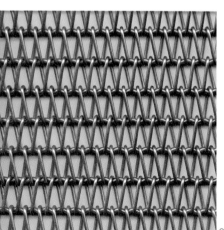

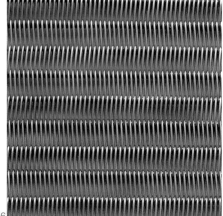

34

35

36

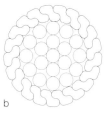

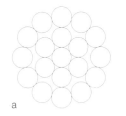

37 a

b

38 c

a

b

d

Wire ropes

DIN 18800 defines two types of high-strength tension members: wire ropes (also often referred to as cables) and those made from prestressing bars. Wire ropes are made from hot-rolled wires that are then cold-drawn. The raw material is killed, cast, unalloyed carbon steel with a carbon equivalent of 0.7%. The microstructure of rolled wire results in a strength of approx. 1000 N/mm². The wire is afterwards subjected to a combined work-hardening and heat-treatment process, so-called patenting. This improves the strength and the surface properties of the final product.

Wire ropes consist of many cold-drawn individual wires. This minimises the frequency of flaws per cross-section compared to monofilament cross-sections (e.g. solid bars). The production of wire ropes is carried out in several steps in a stranding machine. At the start, six wires are wound around a core wire in the direction of a right-hand thread (right lay). In the second step the stranding drum fitted with 12 round bar coilers turns in the direction of a left-hand thread (left lay). This is followed by the next step turning in the opposite direction, and so on. The number of operations corresponds to the number of lays of wire in the rope and determines its final diameter.

particular, structural aspects (changes in length due to temperature fluctuations, wind loads) will require the use of tension springs attached to threaded bars, or hook/eye bars with corresponding fixings to guarantee adequate elasticity and tolerances when under load. Denser fabrics can be trimmed at the top with a flat tensioning bar and screwed to or hung over the underlying construction. Fabrics can be fitted in frames to create movable sunshade elements.

Wire rope types

Generally, the building industry makes use of the following three types of wire rope:

Parallel-wire ropes
These consist exclusively of round wires. They are suitable as guy ropes for antennas and chimneys, as loadbearing and edge cables for lightweight membranes, as the lower chords of timber and steel trusses, as loadbearing and tensioning ropes in cable net constructions, and also for spandrel panels and balustrades.

Locked-coil ropes
The core in this type of wire rope is made up of several lays of round wires. Only the outer lays are formed using Z-wires. These interlocking wire profiles form a smooth, closed surface that prevents infiltration of foreign matter into the inside of the wire rope. The inside of the rope is therefore well protected against corrosion. Locked-coil ropes also offer good resistance to lateral crushing and have a high elastic modulus. They are therefore favoured for external applications and higher loads.

Strand ropes
Owing to their low elastic modulus, their sensitive surface and the lower corrosion resistance, these ropes play only a minor role in the construction industry. Strand ropes consist of one or more lays of strands that are twisted (stranded) like a screw. The strands are very fine ropes made from individual wires whose respective core diameter is max. 800 μm. They are used for moving applications (hoisting and erection ropes, lifts) and for attachment purposes (hangers, slings etc.), i.e. wherever a flexible rope is required. They are also suitable for use in balustrades to stairs, balconies, bridges and walkways.

Corrosion protection for wire ropes

The cold-worked (drawn) steel wire reacts very sensitively to disruptions of the surface (cracks and weld spatter). However, reductions in the size of the cross-section (necking), which only displace the microstructure but do not interrupt it, have hardly any effect on the strength. The surface quality is therefore decisive for the durability of steel wires. Protecting wire ropes against corrosion must be guaranteed through correct installation and protective measures to the wire rope itself.

Corrosion protection through constructional measures
Rainwater must be able to drain away easily from clamp fittings and end anchorages, and ponding avoided by including holes or channels for drainage. Connection details should be arranged so that there is good ventilation to the wire rope and any moisture can evaporate quickly.

Corrosion protection for the individual wires
All individual wires are hot-dip galvanised. The best protection for wires made from unalloyed steel is currently a special protective layer of zinc (95%) and aluminium (5%). Like a normal zinc coating, this is applied by immersing the wire in the molten material. Parallel-wire ropes consist exclusively of round wires coated in this way; rustproof wires represent an alternative. These wires do not have an internal filling. Wire ropes must be regularly maintained and replaced if wires are broken or corrosion is found.

Corrosion protection within locked-coil ropes
The voids between the wires are filled with a suitable lubricant. This filling reduces the internal friction in the rope and forms the internal corrosion protection. The lubricant applied during the stranding of the wires can be squeezed

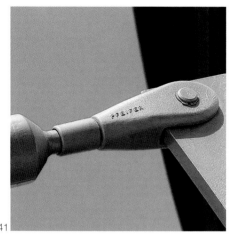

39

40

41

out at the surface of the rope when the rope is loaded. The compatibility of the internal filling with any corrosion protection measures applied to the outside of the wire rope must therefore be checked.

Corrosion protection for the surface of the rope
Particularly corrosive conditions call for an additional coating on the ropes and the end fittings (duplex system). Also when a longer service life or a coloured finish is desired. Corrosion loads, zinc wear rates and a classification of the ambient conditions can be found in DIN EN ISO 12944-2.

Fittings
Cable end fittings
The following end anchorages, thimbles and clamps are approved for high-strength tension members (cables) according to DIN 18800 (see fig. 42):
• Anchorages with metal spelter sockets to DIN EN 13411-4 for
  – parallel-wire ropes
  – locked-coil ropes
  – strand ropes
• Pressed clamps made from wrought aluminium alloys to DIN EN 13411-3 for
  – parallel-wire ropes
  – strand ropes
• Pressed clamps made from steel for
  – parallel-wire ropes
  – strand ropes

In a spelter socket the ends of the wire rope are fanned out and then all grease and foreign matter is cleaned out. The socket is then slipped over the rope and sealed, the whole assembly heated to approx. 400°C and the socket subsequently filled with molten Zamak (a die-casting zinc alloy). If parallel-wire or strand ropes are to be anchored with clamps or thimbles, the ropes must be sufficiently flexible.

Saddles and clips
Cables are particularly heavily loaded at places where they change direction. In order that the transverse compression on the tension member is not excessive, the radius of curvature may not be too small. According to the DIN standards, the radius of the bearing surface of saddles must be equal to at least 20 times the diameter of the cable. Tension members should be properly supported where they change direction. Sharp edges must be avoided.

Tie bar systems

A tie bar system comprises the tie bar itself, the forked end and its fittings (pins, sockets, etc.). The steel used for the tie bar must have a yield stress 30% higher than that of steel grade S355 (which already has a good tensile strength). This enables identical loads to be accommodated with a smaller cross-section, and the tie bar remains slender. Gusset and connecting plates can be made from steel grade S355. Forked end, pin and socket are designed for higher loads than the tie bar itself in order to rule out failure of these components.

Exact adjustment of the length is guaranteed by turning the bar in the left- and right-hand threads of the forked ends; a turnbuckle is therefore not required. The forked end is fixed in place without restraint by a pin hammered into place. When designing and fabricating the connecting plates, care must be taken to adhere to the manufacturer's specification (minimum distances and position of holes). A correct load transfer requires the system axes of all the components connected to intersect at one point. All the parts of a tie bar system should be hot-dip galvanised to DIN EN ISO 1461, or sprayed with zinc to DIN EN 22063.

Threads must be wire-brushed after galvanising. Tie bar systems must carry building authority approval because they are not covered by DIN standards.

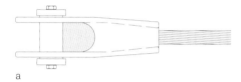

a

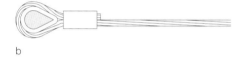

b

42 c

37 a, b Experienced ropemakers are responsible for the accurate fitting of connecting elements to the wire ropes already stretched and cut to length
38 Types of wire rope (cable)
   a Parallel-wire rope
   b Locked-coil rope
   c Strand rope for secondary purposes
   d Bundle of parallel prestressing wires
     Used for straight guy ropes or cast-in tensioning members only because the hexagonal cross-section is unsuitable for changes of direction.
39 Guyed column, saddle for perimeter cable and gusset plate for tie bar connection
40 Parallel-wire ropes with screwed clamps made from cast stainless steel for connecting balustrade rope and suspension rope
41 Approved strut connection
42 Rope end fittings
   a End anchorage with spelter socket
   b Pressed clamp made from wrought aluminium alloy
   c Pressed clamp made from steel

77

Corrosion protection, fire protection, building performance

1 Rusted surface of a steel plate
Rust increases in volume and this can have a knock-on effect for joining components – cracking panes of glass, causing spalling of concrete, or damaging fasteners.

Corrosion protection

Natural iron ore contains iron as a stable oxide. The melting process raises iron and steel to a higher energy level, they become thermodynamically unstable and are always trying to return to the lower energy state. Corrosion is the process of returning the iron atoms to iron oxide in the presence of oxygen and water. Rust forms, a loose composition of low strength. The oxidation results in more mass, the material becomes heavier, the volume expansion leads to stresses, and the rust layer flakes off. The duration of the wet conditions together with the relative humidity and the atmospheric conditions give an indication of the rate of atmospheric corrosion. DIN EN ISO 12944-2 classifies the corrosive conditions in corrosivity categories (see appendix). Also important are the actual moisture relationships on the construction, caused by precipitation, water run-off or condensation. Galvanic corrosion occurs when two metals with different electrochemical potentials are in contact, which results in corrosion of the less noble metal. To prevent this corrosion, surfaces in contact should be isolated with intermediate pads, and in the case of bolts or screws, with plastic washers and sleeves.

Besides impairing the load-carrying capacity of the building components affected (due to a loss of material), corrosion can also damage adjoining components (restraint stresses and spalling due to the increased volume of the corroded steel). Corrosion can also spoil the appearance of a steel structure.

Protection against atmospheric corrosion requires both active and passive measures. Active protection is achieved through designing to prevent corrosion, whereas passive measures protect the steel surface directly. Passive protection includes:
· weathering steel
· stainless steel
· painting
· hot-dip galvanising (coating)
· duplex systems

Designing to prevent corrosion

The surfaces of steel structures should be kept as small as possible and not further subdivided if possible. Building components should be arranged so that they are accessible, so that all surfaces can be prepared and painted manually if necessary, and inspected. Surfaces that will no longer be accessible after erection will require a higher standard of protection. The DIN standard lays down dimensions and limiting values for such cases. Weld seams represent smooth surfaces and should be preferred to riveted or bolted connections, although it must be said that the welding process changes the microstructure of the steel and often makes it more susceptible to corrosion. The pros and cons must be weighed up here as well. Intermittent weld runs and spot welds should be avoided, gaps and slits must be closed off. Hollow sections and other components can be left open or closed off. But the closure to any hollow elements must be so tight that neither air nor moisture can infiltrate (peripheral welds, closure plates). Open hollow sections should always be installed so that they are protected against direct contact with water and adequate ventilation and drainage openings should be included. Protection (e.g. paint) to the internal surfaces may be necessary in some instances. Suitable surface finishes prevent an accumulation of dust, dirt and water, and reduce the rate of corrosion.

Weathering steel

According to DIN EN 10020, weathering steels are classed as stainless steels.

However, they contain fewer alloying constituents (< 1%) and are therefore cheaper. The weather resistance is due to these alloying components, primarily chromium and copper (class W). The addition of phosphorus (0.06–0.15% P) enhances the effect (class WP). Many different grades are available worldwide, and some of these are classified in DIN EN 10155 (new standards are in preparation: EN 10025-5 and 10025-1). The material marketed under the name COR-TEN (characterised by its CORrosion resistance and high TENsile strength) was patented in 1932 in the USA with the alloying constituents copper, phosphorus, silicon, nickel and chromium.

Under normal weather conditions (alternating wet and dry periods), weathering steel forms a protective layer of rust permanently bonded to the underlying surface. This slows down the rusting process but does not stop it entirely. Permanently wet conditions will, however, destroy the protective layer of rust and the steel then begins to corrode like normal steel. The pitting-like corrosion leaves the surface rough. If a more even surface finish is desired, the mill scale caused by the rolling process should be removed by shot-blasting.

Corrosion allowances must be included in the design depending on the planned period of use and the anticipated corrosion loads (C1 to C5-M). ISO 9224-11 specifies corrosion curves for all corrosivity categories. For a planned life of 100 years, the corrosion of weathering steel per surface exposed to the weather is as follows:
· C2 low (rural)   0.11 mm
· C3 moderate (urban)   0.53 mm
· C4 severe (industrial)   1.05 mm
The loss in thickness due to corrosion in the case of weathering steel in category C4 is only half that of unalloyed steel. But unprotected weathering steel is unsuit-

Groups of stainless steels

Microstructure	Code letter	Principal alloying constituents
ferritic	F	Cr
martensitic	M	Cr, C or Ni
austenitic	A	Cr, Ni, Mo
austenitic-ferritic	FA	Cr, Ni, Mo (higher Cr and lower Ni contents than for austenitic steels)

2   3   4

able for category C5 (aggressive industrial, marine). This corrosion rate must be taken account of in the case of loadbearing structures and thin sheets by using thicker material (DASt Directive 007-4). That means more weight, and the structure must be designed accordingly. Weathering steel costs approx. 10–15% more than standard steel. This extra cost can be offset against the cost of providing corrosion protection (initial painting, scaffolding, making good and renewing the paint finish) and also the associated environmental impact (solvents, blasting media).

The above recommendations for designing with corrosion in mind must be adhered to very carefully in the case of weathering steel because the corrosion proceeds at a faster pace here once it has begun. This is especially so in the case of galvanic corrosion (include intermediate pads to separate the steel from more noble metals such as stainless steel, copper, lead, tin and less noble metals like aluminium and zinc/galvanising, prevent scouring, minimise number of bolted connections). DASt Directive 007-4 contains important advice on building properly with weathering steel.

Stainless steel
Stainless steels (to DIN EN 10020) are alloyed and unalloyed steels with a sulphur and phosphorus content of max. 0.035%. A stainless steel is not necessarily a non-rusting steel; to be that, it must have a suitable suffix appended to its name.

Grades
Stainless steels, their classification, properties, forms of supply and applications, are specified in DIN EN 10088 parts 1 to 5. Non-rusting steel with an austenitic microstructure (V2A steel) was produced

for the first time (and patented) in 1912 by alloying with chromium and nickel. Since then, manufacturers and fabricators have been using a whole variety of names such as V2A/V4A, NIROSTA, REMANIT, Chromagan, etc. Today, the term " rustproof stainless steel" covers a group of more than 100 non-corroding, acid-resistant steels. They all contain at least 10.5% chromium (Cr) – the chemical constituent that ensures better corrosion resistance than unalloyed steels. The all-important aspect here is the passive layer rich in chromium oxide that forms on the surface, which, however, still requires an unhindered oxygen exchange to maintain its function. Alloying metals such as nickel and molybdenum can enhance the corrosion resistance. And the addition of further elements (Nb, Ti, N, S) help to influence properties still further. Consequently, every steel producer can produce stainless steels customised to specific applications, which makes classification very complicated. It is therefore important to define in advance which properties the steel should have in the construction (magnetism, weldability, corrosion resistance). Stainless steels are divided into four groups according to chemical composition and microstructure (tab. 4). Ferritic steels can be welded and austenitic varieties are even better for welding, whereas martensitic steels with a high carbon content exhibit only limited suitability. According to building authority approval Z-30.3-6, some 17 stainless steels are approved for use in products, fasteners and building components for loadbearing applications. The most common grades, also for non-loadbearing components, are:
• Nos. 1.4301, 1.4307, 1.4541 basic chromium-nickel steels (formerly V2A)
• Nos. 1.4401, 1.4404, 1.4571 with the addition of molybdenum (formerly V4A)
The individual steel grades are desig-

nated by codes (e.g. X5CrNi18-10) and material numbers (e.g. 1.4301), but often by means of material number only.

Forms of supply
The hot-worked wires and sections plus round, flat, square and profiled bars are rolled or extruded. Their dimensions frequently match those of standard rolled sections made from low-alloy steels; the exact cross-sections available should be checked with the suppliers. Cold-formed sections, beams and tubes with a high stiffness are made from stainless steel sheet by rolling, folding or cold-drawing. Sections are often made to order. Stainless steels can be re-formed just like unalloyed steels, but the forces required are higher owing to the material's higher shear resistance. Manufacturers can supply strips in widths up to 2000 mm and in any length, plus sheets in typical sizes (1000 x 2000, 1250 x 2500, 1500 x 3000 mm). According to DIN EN 10088, three different types of ex works surface finish are possible for strips and sheets: grindable, brushable, bright polished, ground. Surfaces must be protected by plastic sheeting during storage and transport. Grinding, blasting, pickling, passivating, polishing and colouring can be used to improve the surface finish. The smoother the surface, the less susceptible it is to accumulations of dust and dirt, and a smooth surface also improves corrosion resistance. A higher alloy steel may be necessary if a coarser surface finish is desired. Regular cleaning reduces the risk of corrosion, likewise the avoidance of crevices.

2 Roll-profiling of a stainless steel window frame
3 Grinding the welded junction of a stainless steel balustrade to remove tarnishing
4 Groups of stainless steels classified according to their microstructure
5 Applying a paint material through hot melt coating using the airless spraying method
6 Paint system on steel (from top to bottom)
 • corroded steel surface
 • sandblasted corroded surface, quality Sa 2½
 • two coats of rustproofing primer
 • undercoat and finishing coat of rustproofing paint
7 Code letters for paint binders

5

6

Working

Many standard types of welding may be employed, but the particular method employed must be matched to the particular grade of material. Tungsten inert-gas (TIG) welding and plasma arc welding (PAW) with argon are used for thin sheets. After welding, soldering or brazing, all splashes, weld beads and tarnishing must be removed in order to prevent subsequent corrosion. Tarnishing and scale is removed by pickling, which must be followed by good neutralisation and rinsing. Weld seams should be reworked to achieve an even appearance. For the construction sequence on site, it is important that components made from stainless steel are installed at a late stage or, if this is not possible, well protected. Splashes of lime and cement should be removed with a wooden tool preferably before they harden (corrosion risk). Particles of iron from unalloyed steel cause patches of rust on stainless steel, and therefore using the same grinding tools for both materials should be avoided on the building site.

Paint systems

Corrosion protection of steel structures by means of paint systems is covered by DIN EN ISO 12944. Painting is one way of providing passive corrosion protection. The reasons for using paint may be a desire to provide a certain coloured finish, or the fact that the components are too large for hot-dip galvanising. Always refer to the technical information sheets of the manufacturers before carrying out any painting work.

Duration of protection

The prerequisites for a long period of protection are the choice of the right paint system and its correct application. These aspects must be considered depending on the corrosion load of the location and the atmospheric conditions (DIN EN ISO 12944-2), the surface preparation and the required duration of protection. The DIN standards contain tables for this (see appendix). Depending on the type of paint and the aggressiveness of the environment, the duration of protection can vary between 8 and 40 years.

DIN EN ISO 12944-5 specifies film thicknesses for particular periods of protection. The expected duration of protection is not only important from the technical viewpoint, but also a significant economic factor. DIN EN ISO 12944-1 specifies three ranges for duration of protection:
• short (K)   2–5 years
• medium (M)   5–15 years
• long (L)   > 15 years
Specifying the duration of protection helps establish a maintenance programme. The first maintenance measures are normally necessary once the paint system has reached rust scale Ri 3 to DIN ISO 4628-3.

System structure

A paint system comprises a succession of coats applied to a substrate, i.e.
• priming coat
• undercoat
• finishing coat.
The priming coat is both rust preventer and bond enhancer. The rough surface and the adhesion of the film of binder to the metal results in a mechanical bond with the substrate. Priming coats (approx. 60 μm) contain 'active pigments', which stop or delay corrosion chemically and physically. The primers most frequently used are non-leaded zinc oxide, zinc and calcium phosphates plus metallic zinc dust. The latter forms the basis of zinc dust paints.
The undercoat ensures the intended overall thickness of the system. Its protective effect is due to its strength, impermeability and barrier effect.

The finishing coat achieves the desired appearance (coloured, matt, gloss or micaceous) and UV resistance. Optimum application is achieved in the factory by spraying or brushing with liquid paints, or powder-based paints with the addition of heat.

Surface preparation

According to DIN 12944-4, the substrate must be cleaned of all impurities such as mill scale, rust, loose old paint or grease by blasting, pickling or other methods. Described by a standard degree of cleanliness, we distinguish between full or partial preparation. Full preparation means exposing the actual steel surface (quality of preparation: Sa, St, Fl, Be), whereas partial preparation removes only rust and impurities, but leaves intact coatings in place (quality of preparation: Psa, Pst, Pma). A roughness value of 40–80 μm is prescribed for optimum bonding (DIN EN ISO 85031).

Code letters for paint binders

AK	alkyd resin	PF	phenol form-aldehyde resin
AY	acrylic resin		
BIT	bitumen	PMMA	polymethyl methylacrylate
CR	chloroprene rubber		
CTE	epoxy resin tar	PS	polystyrene
CTV	vinyl resin tar	PUR	polyurethane
EP	epoxy resin	PVC	polyvinyl chloride
ESI	ethyl silicate	SB	butadiene-styrene rubber
MF	melamine form-aldehyde resin	SI	silicone rubber
PA	polyamide	UF	urea-form-aldehyde resin
PE	polyethylene	UP	unsaturated polyester resin

7

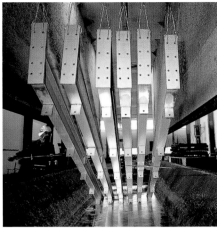

8 Microsection (section through a galvanised surface) showing typical course of hardening of the
iron-zinc alloy layer (from top to bottom)
  • pure zinc Zn
  • iron-zinc alloy layers Fe + Zn
  • steel Fe
9 Several identical components being lifted out of
the hot-dip galvanising tank
10 Classification of galvanising behaviour of structural steels and appearance of ensuing zinc
coating

Types of paint
Paints come in pigmented liquid, paste or
powder forms. They are made up of the
following:
• binders (synthetic resins based on AK,
  AY, PVC, EP, PUR ...)
• active pigments (zinc phosphates, zinc
  dust ...)
• passive pigments (micaceous iron, tal-
  cum …)
• fillers and additives (thickening, anti-
  foaming, anti-sedimentation agents ...)
• solvents (water, organic solvents)

Binders, pigments and fillers form the
actual paint coating after the solvent has
evaporated.
Paints are classified in three main groups
according to type of binder (film formation):
• oxidation-curing (e.g. alkyd resin)
• physically drying (e.g. PVC, acrylic
  resin)
• reactive (two-part products: base +
  activator, e.g. epoxy resin, polyurethane)

Hot-dip galvanising
Hot-dip galvanising (batch galvanising) is
a corrosion protection system applied in
the works under defined conditions
according to DIN EN ISO 1461. The zinc
coating forms an alloy with the steel, is
permanently bonded to it and provides
protection even in the case of abrasion
and scratches. Zinc is less noble than
iron, which means that a galvanic cell is
formed in the presence of a sufficient
amount of moisture (electrolyte). The zinc
functions here as a sacrificial anode. If
the zinc coating is damaged, the sur-
rounding zinc protects the damaged area
against corrosion (cathodic protection).
The hardness of the layer of alloy is
higher than that of normal steels, which
increases the resistance to wear and
abrasion – and that is an advantage over

paint systems during transport, erection
and general use. The total number of
flaws may not exceed 0.5% of the total
surface area of the galvanised component, and no individual damaged area
should be larger than 10 cm^2; otherwise,
re-galvanising will be necessary. Minor
damage can be made good by preparing
the surface and then spraying on a layer
of zinc or zinc dust.
Electrogalvanising of components
immersed in a bath to which an electric
voltage is applied results in only a very
thin layer of protection which is useful for
bolts and screws, but otherwise offers at
best only temporary protection. Contrasting with this, hot-dip galvanising achieves
a coating of zinc that offers long-lasting
protection.
Hot-dip galvanising is carried out in a
bath of molten zinc. At a temperature of
approx. 450°C, a layer of iron-zinc alloy
forms on the surface. The appearance of
this coating depends on the chemical
composition of the steel, the galvanising
conditions (temperature, length of immer-
sion) and the surface finish of the steel.
As the growth of the layer of iron-zinc
alloy depends on the steel composition, it
is virtually impossible for the galvanising
shop to influence this growth. DIN 10025
specifies unalloyed steels that are particularly suitable for galvanising. For example, grade S235, owing to its lower silicon
content, is more suitable for galvanising
than grade S355, but has to be immersed
for a longer time in order to achieve the

necessary coating thickness.
Where steel is to remain exposed, different steel grades or batch changes within
a galvanised construction should be
avoided because the appearance of the
zinc surfaces varies. In order to achieve
an attractive silvery finish, steels with a
silicon and phosphorus content of 0.03%
(No. 1, tab. 10) should be selected, or a
specific alloy for the molten zinc. Steels
complying with the requirements of No. 3
should be preferred for corrosive applications. If the appearance and thickness of
the zinc coating have to satisfy special
demands, these must be agreed first with
the galvanising shop.

Surface preparation
Hot-dip galvanising calls for a bright
metal surface finish. This is achieved in
hydrochloric acid pickling baths with subsequent fluxing. The process removes
grease, rust and mill scale, but impurities
such as old paint, welding residue, slag
and markings must be cleaned off first.

Classification of galvanising behaviour of structural steels

No.	Silicon + phosphorus [%]	Zinc coating
1	< 0.03	Silvery, shiny, spangle pattern, low coating thickness, normal iron-zinc reaction
2	0.03 to < 0.13 Sandelin range	Grey, partly "gritty", high coating thickness, accelerated iron-zinc reaction
3	0.13 to < 0.28 Sebisty range	Silvery and shiny to matt grey, medium coating thickness, normal iron-zinc reaction
4	≥ 0.28	Matt grey, grey appearance as silicon content increases, high coating thickness, accelerated iron-zinc reaction

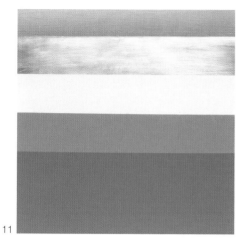

11 Paint system on zinc sheet or galvanised steel
(duplex system), from top to bottom
  · galvanised steel surface
  · surface after washing (grease and chromate
    layer removed with ammonium and wet
    grinding)
  · zinc primer, white
  · undercoat, pigmented to form undercoat
  · finishing coat based on acrylic polyurethane

Duration of protection

The duration of protection provided by a zinc coating is determined by the thickness of the coating and the annual rate of loss. DIN EN ISO 1461 specifies minimum thicknesses depending on the thickness of the steel part. The thickness is specified in micrometres (1 µm = 0.001 mm) and varies between 50 and 150 µm due to the galvanising process. The corrosion rate of zinc is on average approx. 1 µm p.a. High corrosion loads (seawater, industry), long wet periods and the accumulation of impurities can, however, substantially increase annual losses. Classification of corrosivity categories, with rates of loss of zinc and steel, is carried out according to DIN EN ISO 12944-2 (see page 107).

Tenders

As the term "galvanising" covers several methods, tenders and contracts should be based on DIN EN ISO 1461. This is the only way of ensuring permanent corrosion protection. For example, a tender text for hot-dip galvanised and painted construction (duplex system) could read as follows: "Hot-dip galvanising of all steel parts to DIN EN ISO 1461. The steel used must be suitable for hot-dip galvanising and the construction is to be fabricated in a way suitable for hot-dip galvanising. All fasteners such as bolts, nuts, etc. must be hot-dip galvanised to DIN 276-10. Additional paint coatings must comply with DIN EN ISO 12944-5."

Designing for galvanising

Structural steels must be approved for galvanising. Perfect zinc coatings and subsequent adequate corrosion protection are only possible by designing and building in a way that is suited to galvanising. DIN EN ISO 14713 contains recommendations. This is the only way to avoid distortion of the steel parts from the

heat of the molten zinc (450°C), stress cracking or damage. The heat of the bath can also be the reason for the distortion of components with residual stresses due to welding. If a component includes materials of different thicknesses, the individual parts cool at different rates – another cause of distortion. It is then advisable to galvanise the individual components before connecting them.

The bath sizes available also limit the maximum dimensions of components that can be galvanised. Common bath sizes for galvanising are:
· length: approx. 7.00–16.00 m
· width: approx. 1.30–1.90 m
· depth: approx. 1.80–3.20 m

The suspension arrangements for parts to be immersed in the bath should be such that the molten zinc can flow through inlet and outlet holes (frames and hollow sections). It must be possible for the displaced air to escape as well. More zinc collects in drilled holes than on smooth surfaces, and therefore approx. 2 mm play in the holes should be allowed for. The weight also plays a role; the lifting capacities of the cranes in the galvanising shop must be taken into account. Breaking down larger parts into subassemblies should be considered at an early stage. Bulky parts lead to higher costs and whenever possible they should be split into separate, 2D elements which are then assembled after galvanising. Hot-dip galvanised parts can also be welded. However, this vaporises the zinc coating, affects the welding process and ruins the corrosion protection.

Duplex systems

These consist of metallic coating (usually hot-dip galvanising) plus paint finish (DIN EN ISO 1244-5). A duplex system should be chosen when a long period of protection and a coloured finish to the steel components is required. Due to the synergy

effect of the combined corrosion protection measures, the duration of protection can be increased by 1.2–2.5 times the sum of the protection offered by the two systems separately. However, this is the most elaborate and cost-intensive form of corrosion protection.

The zinc coating is protected by the paint finish, which prevents the metallic zinc from being abraded and keeps it in an as-new condition for a long time. The steel remains protected even in the case of local damage to the paint finish, and so rust formation beneath the paint is ruled out. The paint finish lasts longer and problems due to an inadequate coating thickness in voids and recesses, on edges and corners are overcome. The paint must be suitable for applying to a zinc coating (refer to the technical information sheets of the manufacturer).

Good preparation of the surface is important for a functioning duplex system. Depending on the age and condition of the zinc coating, it can be rubbed down wet using an ammonium wetting agent, cleaned with hot-water or high-pressure steam cleaners, ground or sweep-blasted. This last method is a special form of blast-cleaning in which the surface is roughened without damaging it.

The economics of a corrosion protection system are determined by the initial cost plus the cost of maintenance and repair work. When planning corrosion protection, the best costs-benefits ratio should be considered. Short-term protection for structures that have to remain functional for long periods of time is just as wrong as applying expensive long-term measures to structures with a limited lifespan.

Classification of building materials according to their combustibility

Building material	Building materials class to DIN 4102-1	European class to DIN EN 13501-1
incombustible material (e.g. steel, concrete)	A1	A1
incombustible material with combustible constituents (e.g. plasterboard)	A2	A2
not readily flammable material (e.g. oak wood-strip flooring on cement screed)	B1	B
low contribution to fire		C,
flammable material (e.g. timber and wood-based products)	B2	D
acceptable behaviour in fire		E
highly flammable material (e.g. untreated coconut fibre mat)	B3	F

12

13

Fire protection

Temperatures of 1000–1200°C are not uncommon in fires in buildings. Steel is incombustible and consequently does not contribute to fire load or fire propagation. However, steel is a very good conductor of heat; the inside of a steel part heats up quickly and the microstructure of the material is affected. At a temperature of just 500°C, the yield stress drops by two-thirds and the load-carrying capacity is lost. Buildings must be designed so that they remain stable and intact long enough to evacuate persons safely. The building regulations of Germany's federal states contain standardised requirements for duration of fire resistance, building classes (five classes), means of escape and rescue, behaviour of building materials in fire (classes A, B1, B2) and fire walls (compartmentation principle). The model building regulations (MBO), in which the protection of persons and property is defined (cl. 14), forms the basis for these building regulations. The fire resistance class (F 30 to F 180) is specified depending on the use of the building. In order to achieve all this, both planning and constructional measures are necessary.

Planning measures
Fire protection measures relevant to the design are:
- escape routes
- fire compartments (limiting the spread of fire by dividing up the building horizontally and vertically)
- concentrating activities with high fire loads in certain, specially designed sections of the building
- avoiding flashover (spacing of openings, distances to boundaries, fire walls)
- fire brigade access routes
- roof openings (smoke-and-heat vents)
- extinguishing systems (e.g. sprinklers)

Constructional measures
The aim of structural fire protection, as it is called, is to prevent or delay a temperature rise in a steel component. The protective measures employed have an insulating, barrier or heat-dissipating effect. We classify them according to the way they function:
- Transferring the heat build-up to other components with larger mass – achieved by filling hollow columns with concrete (composite construction can achieve fire resistance > F 90), or circulating water (rare); suspended floors with steel trapezoidal profile sheets can be given a concrete topping (composite floors, see page 16).
- Delaying the heat build-up by encasing the steel in concrete, plasterboard or other special boards, or suspended ceilings, intumescent paint or by oversizing the sections (more massive steel sections heat up slower, low ratio of perimeter U to cross-sectional area A).

Exposed steel structures can be possible in certain cases. Simply overdesigning the members can sometimes achieve fire resistance class F 30, especially when using compact sections or when beams are exposed to fire on three sides only. The use of higher strength steels or fire-resistant structural steel (FR 30) is another way of improving fire protection, likewise the use of intumescent paint systems. These systems consist of a primer to protect against corrosion, the coat of intumescent paint itself (0.3–3.5 mm thick depending on fire resistance required) and a finishing coat. At 120–200°C, the intumescent paint foams up and thus forms a heat-insulating layer. Such systems are now available with building authority approvals for up to class F 90, but only in conjunction with open sections with a section factor U/A of max. 160. They are available in very many colours but the

quality of the finished surface is inferior to that of standard paints, and they are considerably more expensive.

Building materials and building components covered by DIN 4102-4 are deemed to comply with the fire resistance requirements. Other building products require building authority approvals or test certificates. In contrast to the German DIN 4102-1classification, the Euronorm series provides greater leeway (DIN EN 13501 parts 1 and 2). Early-warning systems (fire detectors) and immediate fire-fighting measures (sprinklers) protect not only persons and property; their presence may well enable the loadbearing structure to remain unclad because a fully developed fire never ensues. The avoidance of toxic materials that give off dangerous fumes can also help to develop alternatives to the rigid rules of the fire resistance classes – the most frequent cause of death in fires is suffocation by smoke. Taking into account the toxic properties of building materials would therefore make it possible to define sensible fire protection measures in a performance-based method irrespective of the inflexible rules of the descriptive method. Synergies could be exploited because the important stipulations of sound and thermal insulation as well as corrosion protection and architectural requirements can be fulfilled simultaneously.

Fire resistance classes

Fire resistance class	Duration of fire resistance [min]	Building authority designation
F 30	≥ 30	fire-retardant
F 60	≥ 60	fire-retardant
F 90	≥ 90	fire-resistant
F 120	≥ 120	fire-resistant
F 180	≥ 180	highly fire-resistant

14

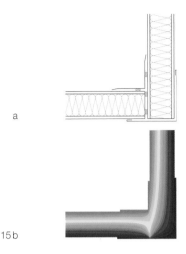

a

15 b

16

12 Classification of building materials according to their combustibility
13 Steel column protected with a layer of intumescent paint, which when it foams up in a fire can attain a thickness of approx. 5 cm, i.e. 40 to 50 times the dry-film thickness, provided this foaming process is not hindered.
14 Fire resistance classes
15 Building envelope made from sandwich panels
   a external corner with inner sheet steel facing penetrating the construction
   b temperature distribution
16 Thermal breaks in steel beams in the plane of the facade (under construction)

Thermal performance

Condensation forms where saturated air cools. Cold air contains little water vapour (e.g. outside = dry air), but hot air contains much more (e.g. inside = high humidity). Once warmer air comes into contact with colder air or is cooled, the vapour condenses to water (temperature below dew point). This can happen on the inside of a building component (inside), but owing to the high temperature gradient in layers of thermal insulation it can also happen within a wall construction, which can lead to saturation.

Steel is a very good heat conductor (λ = 50 W/mK) and therefore easily forms thermal bridges. If steel components penetrate the building envelope, besides the loss of thermal energy, this can sometimes lead to condensation which damages interior fittings and also corrodes the steel components. The formation of condensation is only acceptable in exceptional circumstances. However, even in those cases adequate ventilation and a flow of heat to the steel section should be ensured (see pages 96–97). On no account should such components be simply "wrapped"! The thermal bridge problem can be avoided by enclosing the external steel construction in thermal insulation. Alternatively, the building can be properly conceived from the insulation viewpoint right from the design stage (position of loadbearing structure, insulating concept). One variation is to provide a thermal break in any steel sections penetrating the envelope, as has already become standard for post-and-rail facades. The penetrating beams are interrupted by an intermediate thermal break element. The structural forces are then carried across this "breach" by stainless steel components, whose thermal conductivity (λ = 15 W/mK) is much lower than that of an unalloyed steel.

DIN 4108 prescribes a minimum thermal performance and hence defines upper limits for the thermal transmittance of external components – a certain surface temperature on the inside is thus guaranteed. Calculations according to DIN 4108 for multi-layer components are no longer possible for components incorporating lightweight steel sections. The thermal transmittance should now be worked out roughly according to DIN EN ISO 6946. Determining the heat transfer, surface temperature, checking the risk of condensation and mould growth and optimising the energy-related design of components is frequently only possible through the use of computerised calculations on a 2D or 3D temperature field. The German Energy Conservation Act aims to avoid weaknesses in the construction, e.g. thermal bridges and lack of airtightness, when determining the U-value by incorporating a more favourable coefficient. DIN 4108-6 describes, for example, three methods of assessing the thermal bridges when determining the heating energy requirement.

The correct sequence of layers in a building component avoids damage caused by moisture and large temperature-related movements in loadbearing members. The imperviousness to vapour of the materials must decrease from inside to outside. A vapour barrier or check, a layer with high diffusion resistance and low thermal insulation value (higher thermal conductance) must be placed on the warm side in front of the thermal insulation. Prefabricated facades have a large number of joints and their imperviousness must be considered carefully because water vapour can infiltrate the construction through convection in the joints. The imperviousness can decrease over time (expansion, shrinkage). The design should ensure that any water that does infiltrate can drain away to the outside.

Acoustic performance

The building regulations of Germany's federal states and provisions in DIN 4109 regulate sound insulation in buildings. We distinguish between protection from external noise, the level of which must be reduced to a specified value by the external components, and protection against sound transmissions within a building. What constitutes a reasonable noise level depends on building use and type of occupancy. The degree of airborne sound insulation improves with the mass of the components. Multi-layer, lightweight constructions can achieve sound insulation values equal to those of heavyweight, single-layer constructions when the layers are connected flexibly. The spacing must be large enough to prevent mutual resonance of two neighbouring layers. It is helpful to design them as heavy and non-rigid, and to fill cavities with absorptive materials. All components and their connections, joints and junctions must be impervious. Accurate fit and fewer joints can be achieved through industrial prefabrication – one of steel's advantages. Flanking components can be excited by soundwaves and then transmit this sound to neighbouring rooms. The overall sound insulation of a component is therefore only as good as the insulation between it and its adjoining components. Flanking transmissions must be avoided by interrupting adjoining components.

Besides airborne sound, structure-borne sound, especially impact sound, must also be considered. The latter can be reduced through mass (suspended floor with high weight per unit area), soft floor coverings, floating screeds and/or non-rigid suspended ceilings.

Case studies in steel

Private house in Oldenburg

Architects: LIN Finn Geipel, Giulia Andi,
            Berlin/Paris
Structural Christian Focken,
engineer: Bad Zwischenahn
Completion: 2003

Situated among houses in the typical
north German style in a residential area of
the town of Oldenburg, this minimal steel
box catches the eye. The house was built
for a family with two children and is basi-
cally an industrial shed. In order to meet
the client's demands for ample space on
a tight budget, the architects chose an
inexpensive, prefabricated steel system.
Inside the shed there is a block contain-
ing the standard domestic facilities.
The house is clad with vertical trapezoidal
profile sheeting and stands on a concrete
ground slab that extends 1.5 m beyond
the walls on all four sides. The steel portal
frame made from standard rolled sections
spans the full 9 m width of the building.
Lightweight concrete infill panels provide
the necessary stability for the 22 m long
structure.
On the west side, the living and dining
area occupies the full length and height
of the building. Continuous glazing on
that side enables the interior to be
opened up into the garden. The single-
storey block on the east side contains
kitchen, bathrooms and three small bedrooms in timber studding clad in wood-
based panels and plasterboard. The
access floor beneath this block accom-
modates all the horizontal services to
overcome the need to bury pipes and
cables in the concrete ground slab.
A step running the full length of the building serves as a "corridor zone" linking the
rooms on the east side and the open area
on the west side, and at the same time
houses drawers for storage purposes.
Access to the gallery on top of the single-
storey block is via a mobile steel staircase. The gallery is used by the family as
a quiet zone for reading and working.
Generous glazing at this level allows for
garden views and plenty of daylight.

Section
Plan
scale 1:400

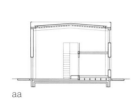

aa

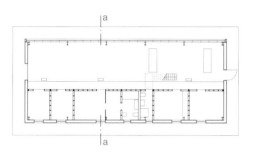

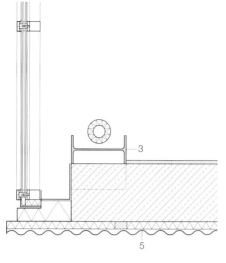

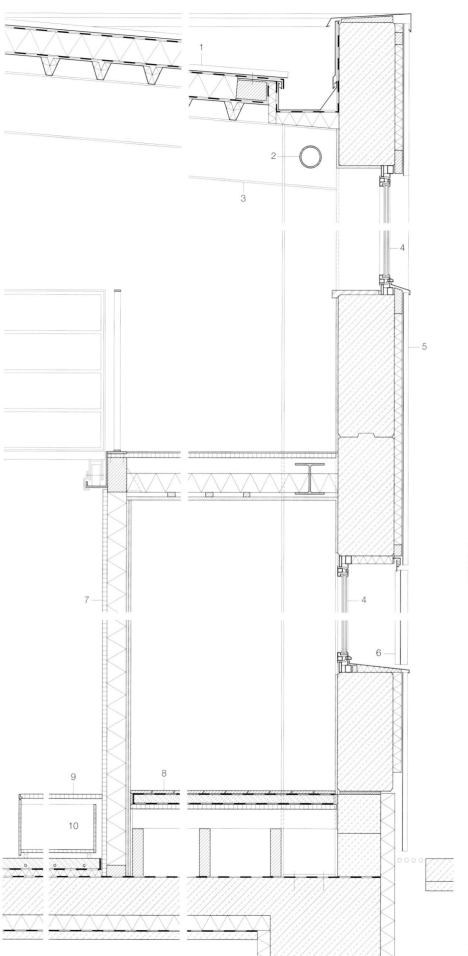

Vertical section,
horizontal section
Glazing
scale 1:20

1   Roof construction:
    42 mm trapezoidal profile sheeting
    waterproofing, 2 layers
    120 mm thermal insulation
    vapour barrier
    100 mm trapezoidal profile sheeting
2   Steel circular hollow section, Ø 120 mm
3   Steel rafter, IPE 300
4   Opening light: insulating glass (6 mm float glass
    + 15 mm cavity + 6 mm toughened safety glass)
    in aluminium frame
5   Wall construction:
    18 mm corrugated sheeting
    framing, 40 x 60 mm battens
    40 mm thermal insulation
    300 mm lightweight concrete
    10 mm plaster
6   Folding shutters
    18 mm corrugated sheeting, perforated
7   Partition construction:
    25 mm chipboard
    100 mm timber studding
    100 mm thermal insulation
    2 No. 12.5 mm plasterboard
8   Access floor construction:
    15 mm wood-strip flooring, separating layer
    45 mm screed
    waterproofing, 25 mm chipboard
    framing, 60 x 100 mm joists
9   Step: 2 mm linoleum
    25 mm chipboard
    aluminium angle edge trim
    framing, 60 x 100 mm joists
10 Drawer, 12 mm chipboard

89

**Pretensioned strip bridge in the
Via Mala gorge**

Location plan
scale 1:750
Vertical sections
scale 1:20

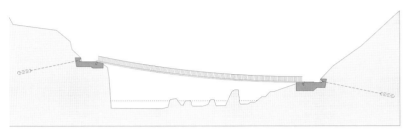

Architects/   Conzett, Bronzini,
Structural   Gartmann Ingenieure,
engineers: Chur (CH)
Completion: 1999

The Punt da Suransuns spans a 40 m wide gorge near the source of the Rhine and forms part of the Via Mala path. In addition, it overcomes a difference in level of approx. 4.0 m and leaves a large clear opening beneath the bridge.
The bridge is not much more than four stainless steel strips and a deck of stone slabs. In structural terms it functions similarly to a suspension bridge, with the stone deck serving as both suspension cable and stiffening beam.
The steel plates holding the ends of the steel strips in place are cast into massive concrete abutments at both ends. The

precision of the components was checked constantly during manufacture. A helicopter transported each relatively lightweight steel strip to the site in one piece; only two flights were necessary. After fixing the steel strips, the Andeer gneiss stone slabs were laid starting at the lower abutment. The slabs are fixed to the stainless steel strips by way of the balustrade. However, the nuts were not fully tightened at first. As the steel strips were pretensioned, the stone slabs and the 3 mm thick aluminium plates in between (instead of mortar) were pressed together in such a way that they became

wedged together. This permanent "bond" means that the construction acts like an arch bridge turned upside down. After creating this bond, the nuts to the balustrade were finally tightened and the handrails welded to the tops of the uprights on site. All the steel parts are made from high alloy V4A chromium-nickel steel because the bridge is affected by the deicing salts used on the trunk road that crosses the gorge at a higher level.

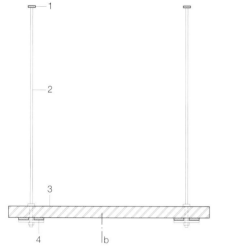

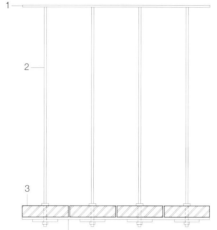

Vertical section
scale 1:20

1 Stainless steel handrail, 10 x 40 mm,
   welded on site
2 Uprights, Ø 16 mm
3 Stone slabs, Andeer gneiss, 1100 x 250 x 60 mm
4 Stainless steel strip, 15 x 60 x 42 966 mm
5 Aluminium strip in joint, 3 x 60 x 1100 mm
6 Hook
7 Temporary hydraulic jack, 500 kN
8 Anchorage for temporary pretensioning
   equipment
9 Reinforced concrete abutment anchored
   to the rock

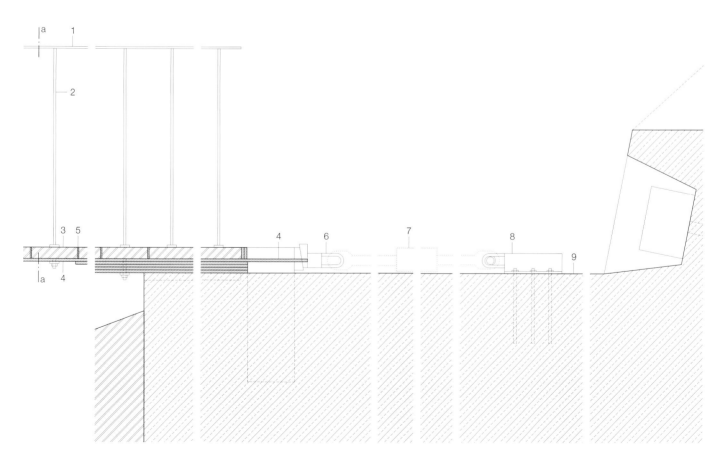

Additional storey in Stuttgart

Architects: Hartwig N. Schneider Architekten,
Stuttgart
Gabriele Schneider, Hartwig Schneider
Structural Hugo Rieger,
engineer: Eckenthal-Brand
Completion: 2003

The removal of a hipped roof from a low-cost apartment block dating from the 1950s and its replacement by a new glazed rooftop storey has resulted in a platform that seems to float above the city. Both the clearance zones and also the building authority's stipulation of a set-back storey have been realised. The existing building was refurbished as part of the same project. The glazing to all sides creates the impression of an open rooftop terrace, even from inside. Six 1.90 m wide external sliding doors with untreated aluminium frames guarantee a level transition to the outdoor rooftop terrace and ensure adequate cross-ventilation, which in summer enables rapid cooling of the lightweight rooftop structure. They remain closed in the winter when a controlled ventilation system minimises heat losses. Below the existing second storey there are small bed-sit apartments dominated by the 3.75 m grid of the box frame construction and accessed via an external walkway. The second storey can form part of the rooftop apartment or can be used separately as an office. Both rooftop apartment and second storey are reached via a separate external spiral staircase. Low weight was an essential criterion for the additional storey and therefore the minimised structure consists of industrial semi-finished products: the steel facade posts also support the roof, the soffit of which is formed by trapezoidal profile sheets spanning 6 m without intermediate supports. The 750 mm wide sheets are connected at the side laps with shear-resistant rivet fasteners, thus creating a stiff horizontal diaphragm at roof level which is supported on a steel angle perimeter beam.

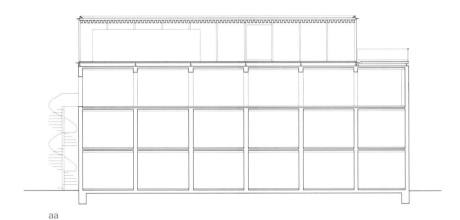

aa

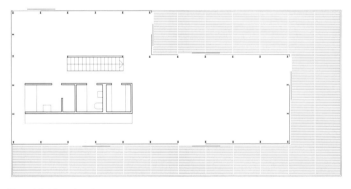

Plan of 3rd floor (new)

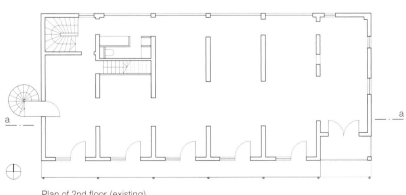

Plan of 2nd floor (existing)

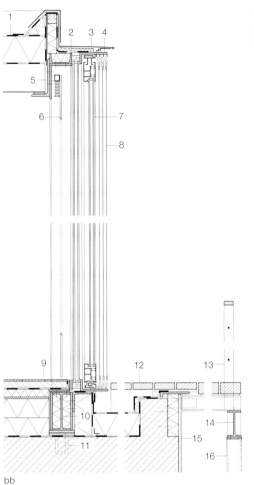

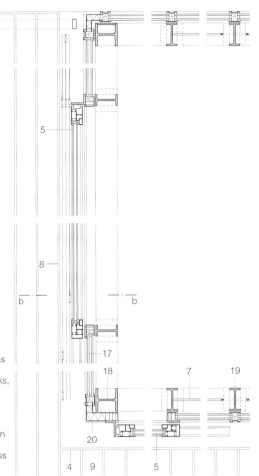

Plans, section
scale 1:250
Vertical section, horizontal section
scale 1:20

1 Roof construction:
  waterproofing
  140 mm thermal insulation
  vapour barrier
  trapezoidal profile sheeting,
  160 x 250 x 1.5 mm
2 Top chord to facade frame, 120 mm
  steel channel
3 Aluminium composite sheet, 4 mm
4 Aluminium angle, 150 x 60 x 10 mm
5 Perimeter beam,
  200 x 100 x 15 mm steel angle
6 Wind bracing, Ø 20 mm steel bar
7 Sliding door, insulating glass
  (6 mm + 12 mm cavity + 6 mm)
  in aluminium frame
8 Fabric sunblind, silver
9 Floor construction:
  20 mm oak floorboards
  40 mm screed
  separating layer
  40 mm impact sound insulation
  2 No. 100 mm thermal insulation
  vapour barrier
  200 mm reinforced concrete (existing)
10 Steel section, IPE 200
11 Base plate, 140 x 100 x 15, with
  40 x 40 x 100 mm steel hollow section as
  shear connector
12 Terrace floor covering, Douglas fir planks,
  110 x 60 mm
13 Balustrade, 50 x 20 mm steel flats
14 Terrace beam, 142 mm steel I-section
15 Coloured render, 15 mm, on existing
16 Column, 80 x 60 mm steel hollow section
17 Fixed light, 8 mm tough. safety glass +
  12 mm cavity + 8 mm tough. safety glass
18 Corner column, HEA 120 steel section
19 Facade post, IPE 120 steel section
20 Aluminium panel, 50 mm

bb

Private house with medical practice in Saulgau

Architect: Ingo Bucher-Beholz, Gaienhofen
Structural engineer: Helmut Fischer, Bad Endorf
Completion: 1999

This building in Saulgau stands with its gables facing the slope and has large areas of glazing providing views across the valley. The three-storey building, with space for a medical practice in the basement, consists of a steel frame with timber infill panels. The simple form of the building envelope presents an exciting contrast to the precisely detailed steel structure.

The steel hollow section loadbearing columns supported on the reinforced concrete ground slab measure just 70 x 70 mm. Positioned every 2 m, these carry the steel floor beams (IPE 140 sections), which are secured with bolts. The 2.0 x 4.0 m grid is hence established by this minimal loadbearing construction. The suspended floors spanning between the floor beams consist of 50 mm thick 3-ply core plywood on which a floating screed has been laid. The walls consist of alternate panels of thermally insulated timber frames with 3-ply core plywood on the outside and large-format fixed glazing. The timber and glass are fixed in the same plane and the only texture is provided by the narrow, off-the-shelf aluminium facade cover strips. Cantilevering balconies, walkways and stairs in galvanised steel create relief. Inside the building, the structural steelwork has been left exposed because in this class of building it does not require any fire-resistant cladding. The interior is broken up by dry-lining partitions plus full-height doors and openings.

Plans, section
scale 1:200

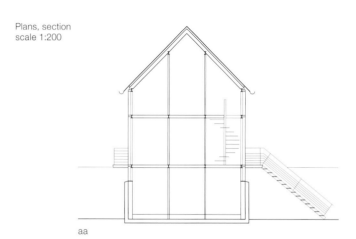

aa

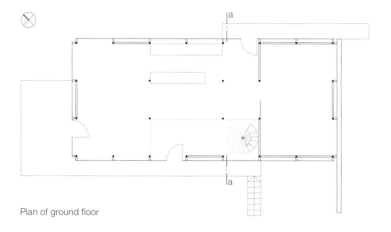

Plan of ground floor

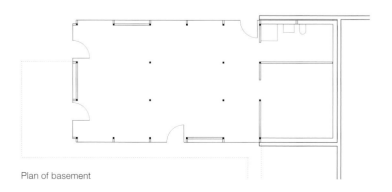

Plan of basement

94

Vertical section
scale 1:20

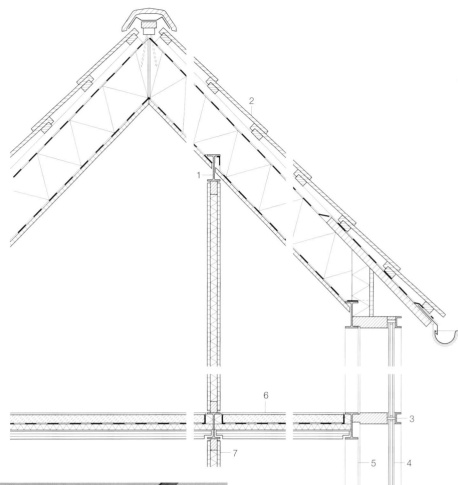

1   Steel purlin, IPE 140 section
2   Roof construction:
    concrete roof tiles
    30 x 50 mm tiling battens
    40 x 60 mm counter battens
    roofing felt, open to diffusion
    70 x 220 mm rafters
    220 mm mineral thermal insulation between rafters
    PE sheeting
    19 mm chipboard
3   Aluminium cover strip, 50 x 20 mm channel
4   Insulating glass, 6 mm + 16 mm cavity + 6 mm
5   Steel column, 70 x 70 x 4 mm hollow section
6   Floor construction:
    3 mm linoleum
    60 mm heated screed
    PE sheeting
    30 mm thermal insulation
    50 mm 3-ply core plywood, glazed finish
7   Partition construction:
    16 mm chipboard
    60 x 40 mm timber frame
    40 mm thermal insulation between members
    16 mm chipboard
8   Floor construction:
    10 mm floor covering
    50 mm screed
    PE sheeting
    30 mm thermal insulation
    2 No. 80 mm thermal insulation
    200 mm reinforced concrete

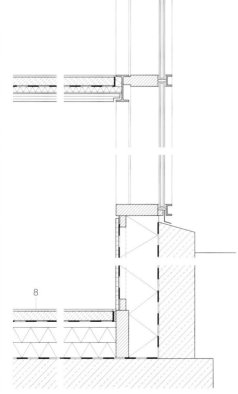

Restaurant and casino in Dresden

Architects: Auer + Weber + Partner, Stuttgart
Structural Ingenieurbüro Mayr + Ludescher,
engineers: Stuttgart
Completion: 1998

This long pavilion-type building with fully glazed ground floor is situated in park-like surroundings. The foyer divides the ground floor into restaurant and casino, with kitchen and ancillary rooms located in the basement. Daylight entering the rooflights highlights certain areas and changes the interior atmosphere depending on time and weather conditions.

A beam grid with moderate spans (5.25 x 10.50 m) has been erected above the reinforced concrete basement. The slender solid-web IPE 330 members were split into transportable segments at the works. Once on site, they were lifted onto the columns and welded together. A multi-coat paint system with a micaceous iron oxide finishing coat protects the entire steel construction against corrosion. Internal steel members have been given an additional F 30 intumescent paint finish. The structure is stabilised by way of X-bracing in the facade and reinforced concrete cores. Ribbed wood-based boards, connected to the beam grid by means of shear-resistant fasteners, span across the building and lend the roof plate the necessary stability. The voids between the ribs are used to evenly distribute the incoming fresh air, while exposed ducts below the ceiling distribute the fresh air in the longitudinal direction. Plywood louvres on the underside of the roof construction optimise the interior acoustics. To achieve more transparency, the horizontal facade elements made from laminated veneer lumber (LVL) are suspended on stainless steel bars from the primary structure, which makes vertical posts superfluous. Wind loads are transferred directly to the steel columns behind the facade. The steel structure therefore remains visible and emphasizes the fine scale of this building. Movable sunshades vary the external appearance.

96

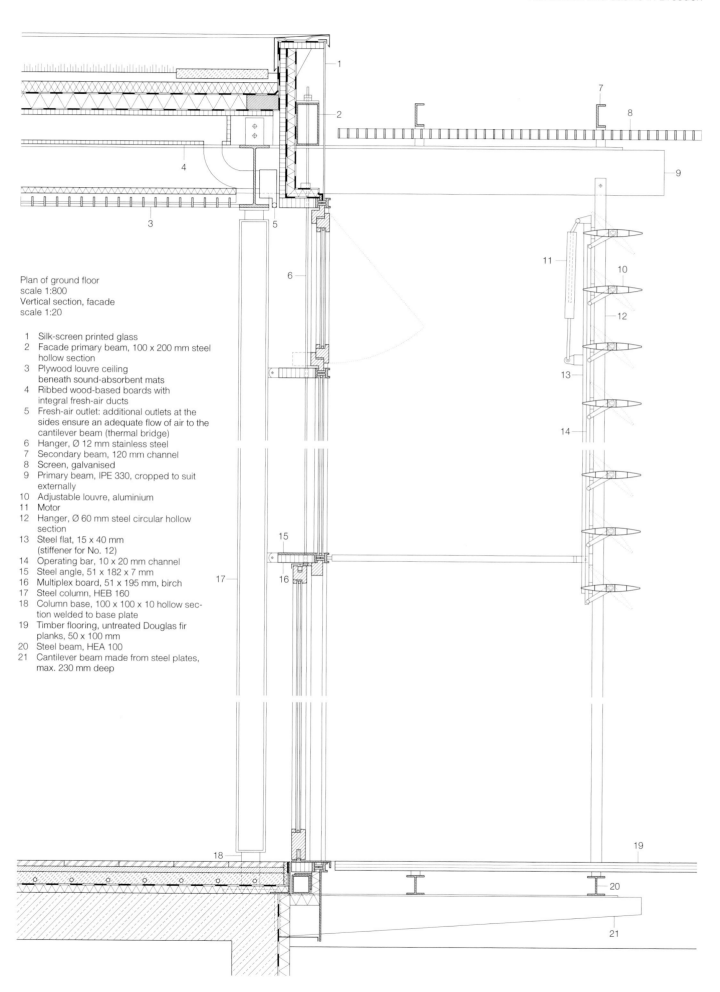

Plan of ground floor
scale 1:800
Vertical section, facade
scale 1:20

1 Silk-screen printed glass
2 Facade primary beam, 100 x 200 mm steel
   hollow section
3 Plywood louvre ceiling
   beneath sound-absorbent mats
4 Ribbed wood-based boards with
   integral fresh-air ducts
5 Fresh-air outlet: additional outlets at the
   sides ensure an adequate flow of air to the
   cantilever beam (thermal bridge)
6 Hanger, Ø 12 mm stainless steel
7 Secondary beam, 120 mm channel
8 Screen, galvanised
9 Primary beam, IPE 330, cropped to suit
   externally
10 Adjustable louvre, aluminium
11 Motor
12 Hanger, Ø 60 mm steel circular hollow
    section
13 Steel flat, 15 x 40 mm
    (stiffener for No. 12)
14 Operating bar, 10 x 20 mm channel
15 Steel angle, 51 x 182 x 7 mm
16 Multiplex board, 51 x 195 mm, birch
17 Steel column, HEB 160
18 Column base, 100 x 100 x 10 hollow sec-
    tion welded to base plate
19 Timber flooring, untreated Douglas fir
    planks, 50 x 100 mm
20 Steel beam, HEA 100
21 Cantilever beam made from steel plates,
    max. 230 mm deep

Conversion of mine building
in Peißenberg

This former mine building dating from 1874/75 and protected by a preservation order has been refurbished and converted into a public building with theatre and mining museum.

Besides the careful overhaul of the existing structure, substantial new works were also involved. The old machine halls consist of 400 mm thick clay brickwork and reinforced concrete walls in the basement. The roof is supported by approx. 3.0 m deep riveted trusses spanning about 14.5 m. As the loadbearing structure could not be verified in accordance with current codes of practice, it had to be strengthened and approved in a special separate procedure. The strengthening takes the form of barely visible batten plates fitted between the individual struts of the trusses. The new mezzanine floors in all the buildings are made from steel I-sections in an orthogonal layout, with columns and beams employing the same steel sections on an approx. 3.50 m grid. In situ concrete, 160 mm thick, has been used for the floors. Bracing of the structural steelwork has been achieved by designing the frame corners as rigid connections.

Architects: Reichel Architekten, Kassel
Müller-Hamann, Architect, Munich
Structural Ingenieurbüro Handel,
engineers: Weilheim
Completion: 2004

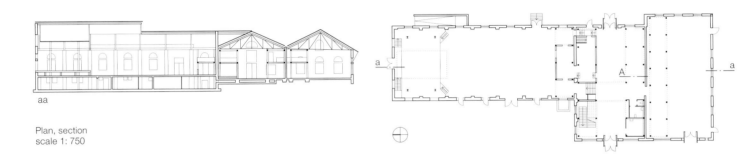

aa

Plan, section
scale 1: 750

Vertical section
scale 1:20
1 Roof construction:
 10 mm Eternit corrugated sheets
 40 x 60 mm battens
 30 x 50 mm counter battens
 roofing felt
 40 mm air cavity
 160 mm mineral fibre thermal insulation
 vapour barrier
 24 mm boarding, glazed finish to underside
2 Steel purlin, HEA 140
3 Historical truss consisting of
 2 No. 100 x 65 mm angles
4 Steel beam, HEB 160
5 Balustrade:
 30 x 8 mm steel flats
 zinc phosphate priming coat
 micaceous iron oxide finishing coat, anthracite
6 Mezzanine floor construction:
 2 coats of transparent varnish
 160 mm reinforced concrete
 100 x 200 mm board formwork
7 Existing masonry, 250 mm
8 Ground floor construction:
 2 coats of transparent varnish
 72 mm heated screed, reinforced
 35 mm impact sound insulation
 50 mm thermal insulation
 PE sheeting
 150 mm reinforced concrete
 50 mm blinding
9 Polycarbonate sheet, lit from behind

A

Private house in Dornbirn

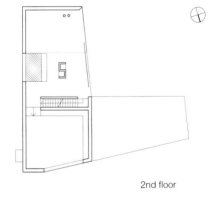

Architects: Oskar Leo Kaufmann,
               Albert Rüf, Dornbirn
Structural   Norbert Gsteu,
engineer: Feldkirch
Completion: 2002

Sections, plans
scale 1:400

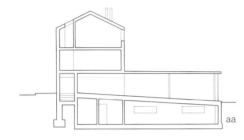

aa

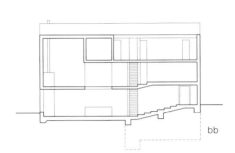

bb

This metal-clad house is located in Dornbirn, the largest town in the Austrian province of Vorarlberg. Steel is used here, not structurally, but as the material for the building envelope. Perforated stainless steel plates cover the entire building almost seamlessly and present a completely closed face on the street side. The duopitch roof is the sole allusion to the neighbouring buildings. Rainwater passes through the perforated plates and drains away on a layer of coated polyester fleece behind the stainless steel. On the roof surfaces, additional battens beneath the fleece help reduce the noise level during rainfall.

The main entrance is directly on the street. From this entrance, stairs lead down to the open-plan kitchen and living room at a lower level. This is where the image of the introverted structure is reversed: a 9 m wide, full-height window links the interior with the garden. The appearance of the interior is, like the exterior, very homogeneous. Fair-face concrete walls and soffits dominate the living quarters. The wooden window frames represent a stark contrast to these cool surfaces, and warmer colours also dominate the top floor, which features timber walls and roof with a poplar veneer finish. A corridor lined with cupboards provides access to the bedrooms, where overhead glazing in the plane of the perforated roof plates permits an unobstructed view of the sky.

1st floor

2nd floor

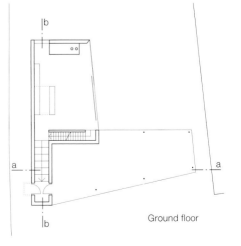

Ground floor

Basement

Vertical section
scale 1:20

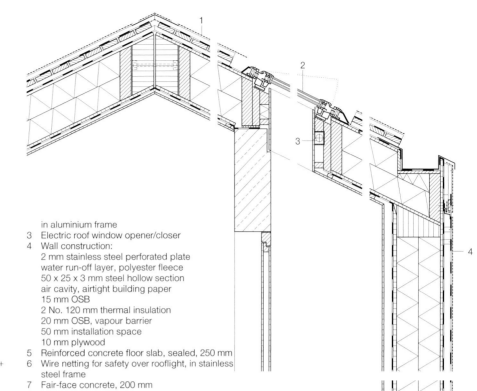

1 Roof construction:
   2 mm stainless steel perforated plate
   50 x 25 x 3 mm steel hollow section
   air cavity, airtight building paper
   90 x 25 mm timber boards on battens
   waterproofing
   15 mm OSB
   240 x 100 mm glulam rafters
   2 No. 120 mm mineral wool thermal insulation
   between rafters
   15 mm OSB, vapour barrier
   20 x 50 mm battens
   10 mm plywood, poplar veneer facing
2 Insulating glass: 6 mm toughened safety glass +
   16 mm cavity + 6 mm laminated safety glass
   (2 No. toughened safety glass panes)

   in aluminium frame
3 Electric roof window opener/closer
4 Wall construction:
   2 mm stainless steel perforated plate
   water run-off layer, polyester fleece
   50 x 25 x 3 mm steel hollow section
   air cavity, airtight building paper
   15 mm OSB
   2 No. 120 mm thermal insulation
   20 mm OSB, vapour barrier
   50 mm installation space
   10 mm plywood
5 Reinforced concrete floor slab, sealed, 250 mm
6 Wire netting for safety over rooflight, in stainless
   steel frame
7 Fair-face concrete, 200 mm

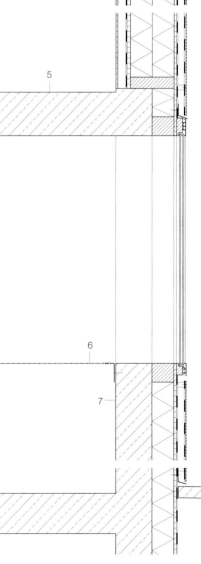

Hinzert documentation pavilion

Architects: Wandel Hoefer Lorch + Hirsch,
           Saarbrücken, Frankfurt
Structural   Schweitzer Ingenieure,
engineers: Saarbrücken
Completion: 2005

Hinzert in Hunsrück is surrounded by an idyllic landscape. There are virtually no signs of the horrors that took place here between 1939 and 1945 when this was the site of a concentration camp in which more than 13,000 people were mal-treated. In order that the less well-known Hinzert concentration camp and its pris-oners should never be forgotten, a com-petition for a documentation pavilion was initiated. The winning design with its self-supporting envelope of welded Cor-Ten steel plates has a glass facade at the end facing the former camp. Printed on the glass – seemingly superimposed on the landscape – is an archive photograph of the prisoners' barracks. The building envelope is loadbearing structure and facade all in one; it needs no further structural elements or cladding. More than 3,000 triangular Cor-Ten steel plates, every one different and prepared on a CNC milling machine, were assembled in the factory to form 12 large-format ele-ments which were then welded together on site. The angles between the individual plates are chosen so that the elements have an adequate structural depth and the whole construction forms a folded plate structure with sufficient stability. After welding, the surface of the steel was sand-blasted and evenly pre-oxidised. Subsequent treatment with hot paraffin lends additional relief and a semi-gloss finish.

The interior is dominated by timber lining to the walls and soffits, also divided into triangular panels. Texts and images describing the history of the camp are printed directly on the wooden wall sur-faces of the exhibition hall. The few origi-nal documents still in existence are dis-played in glass showcases embedded in the walls. The exhibition is a much-needed visual continuation of the memo-ries that up until now had been handed down by word of mouth only.

Plan, sections
scale 1:500
Wire model
vertical section, horizontal section
scale 1:20

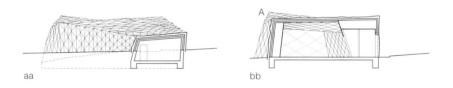

aa   bb

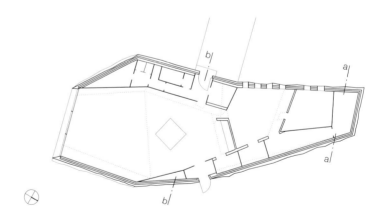

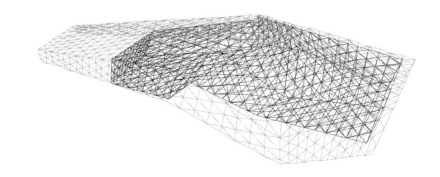

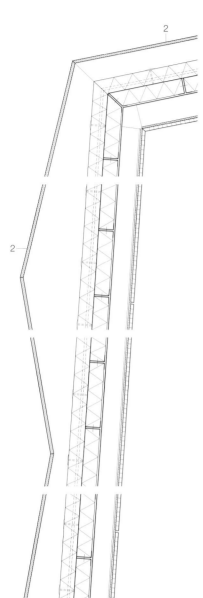

1   Void filled with ballast
2   Envelope construction:
    14 mm pre-oxidised steel sheet,
    hot paraffin treatment
    95–300 mm air cavity
    80 mm mineral fibre thermal insulation,
    hydrophobic coating
    80 mm sheet steel pan,
    with thermal insulation
    vapour barrier,
    1.5 mm stainless steel sheet
    95 mm installation space, cold-worked
    sections
    wood-based board,

plasterboard to rear,
or perforated with
sound-attenuating fleece to rear,
17 mm birch veneer on visible side
3   Aluminium sheet, 3 mm
4   Opening light:
    insulating glass (8 mm laminated safety glass +
    14 mm cavity + 6 mm toughened safety glass) in
    aluminium frame
5   Thermal break

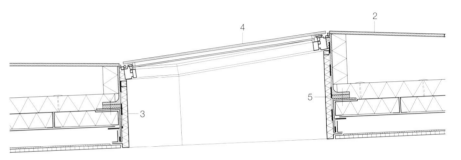

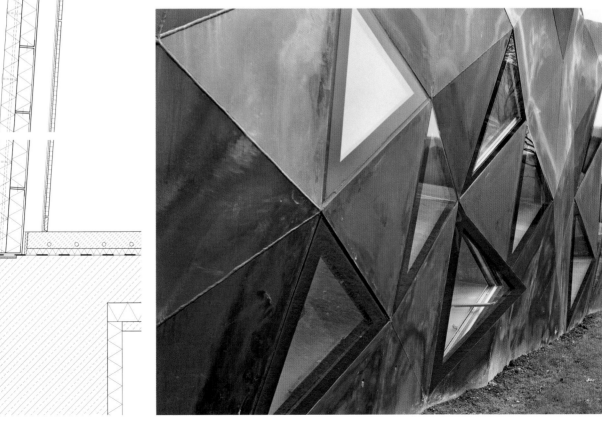

A

Designations and properties of structural steels

Type	Material designation			Tensile strength[1] [N/mm²]	Min. yield stress[3] [N/mm²]	Min. elongtion at rupture[5] $L_0 = 5 d_0$ [%]
	to EN 10027-1 and CR 10260	to former EN 10027-2 and CR 10260	German designation			
	S185[2]	1.0035	St 33	290–510	185	18
General structural steels to DIN EN 10025	S235JR	1.0037	St 37-2	340–470	235	26
	S235JRG1	1.0036	USt 37-2			
	S235JRG2	1.0038	RSt 37-2			
	S235JO	1.0114	St 37-3U		235[4]	
	S235J2G3	1.0116	St 37-3N			
	S235J2G4	1.0117	–			
	S275JR	1.0044	St 44-2	410–560	275	22
	S275JO	1.0143	St 44-3U			
	S275J2G3	1.0144	St 44-3N			
	S275J2G4	1.0145	–			
	S255JR	1.0045	–	490–630	355	22
	S255JO	1.0553	St 52-3U			
	S255J2G3	1.0570	St 52-3N			
	S255J2G4	1.0577	–			
	S255K2G3	1.0595	–			
	S255K2G4	1.0596	–			
	E295	1.0050	St 50-2	470–610	295	20
	E335	1.0060	St 60-2	570–710	335	16
	E295	1.0070	St 70-2	690–830	360	11
High-strength weldable fine-grained structural steels to DIN EN 10113 T2[6]	S275N	1.0490	StE 285	370–510[7]	275[8]	24
	S275NL	1.0491	TStE 285			
	S355N	1.0545	StE 355	470–630[7]	355[8]	22
	S355NL	1.0546	TStE 355			
	S420N	1.8902	StE 420	520–680[7]	420[8]	19
	S420NL	1.8912	TStE 420			
	S460N	1.8901	StE 460	550–720[7]	460[8]	17
	S460NL	1.8903	TStE 460			
Hollow sections for structural steelwork[9]	S235JRH	1.0039	RSt 37-2	340–470[11]	235	26
	S275JOH	1.0149	St 44-	410–560[11]	275	22
	S275J2H	1.0138	St 44-3			
	S355JOH	1.0547	St 52-3U	490–630[11]	355	21
	S355J2H	1.0576	St 52-3N			
	S275NH	1.0493	StE 285	370–510[11]	275[12]	24
	S275NLH	1.0497	TStE 285			
	S355NH	1.0539	StE 355	470–630[11]	355[12]	22
	S355NLH	1.0549	TStE 355			
	(S420)[10]		(StE 420)	(500–660)	(420)	(19)
	S460NH	1.8953	StE 460	550–720[11]	460[12]	17
	S460NLH	1.8956	TStE 460			

[1] Valid for product thicknesses > 3 to ≤ 10 mm. Higher values apply to smaller thicknesses. The values are reduced by 10 to 50 N/mm² for thicknesses from 100 to 250 mm.

[2] Available in nominal thicknesses ≤ 25 mm only.

[3] Valid for thicknesses up to 16 mm. The values are reduced by 10 N/mm² for thicknesses > 16 to ≤ 40 mm, and by 20 N/mm² for thicknesses > 40 to ≤ 63 mm. The values are reduced by a further 10 N/mm² for each of the following steps: > 63 to ≤ 80 mm, > 80 to ≤ 100 mm, > 100 to ≤ 150 mm, > 150 to ≤ 200 mm and > 200 to ≤ 250 mm. For exceptions see note[5].

[4] The value for thicknesses > 40 to ≤ 100 mm is 215 N/mm².

[5] These values apply to longitudinal test pieces for product thicknesses ≥ 3 to ≤ 40 mm. Lower values apply to transverse test pieces as well as lesser and greater thicknesses.

[6] DIN EN 10113-3 is valid for thermomechanically rolled steels. Such grades are given the code letter M (instead of N).

[7] Valid for thicknesses up to 100 mm.

[8] Valid for thicknesses up to 16 mm. The values are reduced by 10 to 60 N/mm² for greater thicknesses.

[9] These values apply to hot-finished hollow sections to DIN EN 10210-1 (Sept 1994 ed.) and cold-finished welded hollow sections to DIN EN 10219-1 (1997 ed.). DIN EN 10219-1 contains additional stipulations for sections with the designations ...MH and ...MHL (thermomechanical treatment of primary products).

[10] Only in DIN EN 10219 in supply conditions MH and MLH.

[11] Valid for thicknesses ≥ 3 to ≤ 65 mm, or max. 40 mm for cold-finished hollow sections.

[12] Valid for thicknesses up to 16 mm. The values are reduced by 10 N/mm² for thicknesses > 16 to ≤ 40 mm, and by 20 N/mm² for thicknesses > 40 to ≤ 65 mm.

Sections according to international standards

Not standardised	Not covered by Euronorms (sections to international standards)	Abbreviation
Wide I-beams (extra light)		HE-AA
Wide-flange beams	works standard, Arbed section, Lux.	HL
Wide-flange column sections	ditto, ASTM A6/A6M – 90a	HD
Wide-flange piles	ditto	HP
American wide-flange beams	ASTM A6/A6M – 6–44	W
British universal beams	BS 4 178–914	UB
British universal columns	BS 4 152–356	UC
Parallel-flange channels	NF A 45–225	UAP
Japanese sections	JIS 100-500 to JIS G3192	JIS

Bolts and screws to DIN 7990 and *DIN 6914*: dimensions and minimum pitches for erection purposes

Bolt/screw size		M 12	M16	M 20	M22	M24	M 27	M30	M 36
Thread dia.	d	12	16	20	22	24	27	30	36
Shank dia.	d_s				= thread dia. d				
ditto, close-tolerance bolt	d_s	13	17	21	23	25	28	31	37
Head depth	k	8	10	13	14	15	17	19	23
Nut depth max. m		12.2	15.9	19.0	20.2	22.3	24.7	26.4	31.5
		10	*13*	*16*	*18*	*19*	*22*	*24*	*29*
Distance across flats (AF)	s	18	24	30	34	36	41	46	55
		22	*27*	*32*	*36*	*41*	*46*	*50*	*60*
Distance across corners min. e		19.85	26.17	32.95	37.29	39.55	45.20	50.85	60.79
		23.91	*29.56*	*35.03*	*39.55*	*45.20*	*50.85*	*55.37*	*66.44*
Washer dia.		24	30	37	39	44	50	56	60
		24	*30*	*37*	*39*	*44*	*50*	*56*	*66*
Washer thickness	t	8	8	8	8	8	8	8	8
		3	*4*	*4*	*4*	*4*	*5*	*5*	*6*

All dimensions in mm. Where only one figure is given, this applies to both standards.
The minimum pitches were determined from tool details supplied by the Hoffmann Group. These figures may vary when using the tools of other manufacturers.
Bolts and screws to DIN 7990. *In italics: bolts and screws to DIN 6914.*

Using an open-ended spanner

Bolt/screw size		M 12	M16	M 20	M22	M24	M 27	M30	M 36
	b_1	43	53	70	75	80	88	94	
		49	*60*	*70*	*80*	*88*	*94*		
	max. h	8	10	10	11	14	14	14	
	max. L	250	300	325	375	425	425	425	

Radius r necessary for turning the head of the spanner about the axis of the bolt/screw (the length L of the spanner must be considered as well in the case of a 360° rotation):

		M 12	M16	M 20	M22	M24	M 27	M30	M 36
		51.0	67.3	83.6	94.5	99.9	113.5	127.1	
		61.8	*75.4*	*89.0*	*99.9*	*113.5*	*127.1*		

These values are based on various turning positions and include a safety allowance of 2 mm.

Using a socket spanner

Bolt/screw size		M 12	M16	M 20	M22	M24	M 27	M30	M 36
	D	25	32.3–34.5	39.9–42	44.6–47	49.5	55.5–59	61–65	72–76
		29.9–32	*36.2–38.5*	*42.4–44.5*	*49.5*	*55.5–59*	*61–65*	*66*	*78–82.5*
	L	38	52/90	58/90	60/90	60/90	67/90	73	80
		52/90	*55/90*	*58/90*	*60/90*	*67/90*	*73*	*80*	*80*

Radius r necessary for turning the ratchet head of the spanner about the axis of the bolt/screw (socket is critical for M 36):

		M 12	M16	M 20	M22	M24	M 27	M30	M 36
		37.0	37.0	37.0	37.0	37.0	37.0	37.0	40.0
		37.0	*37.0*	*37.0*	*37.0*	*37.0*	*37.0*	*37.0*	*43.3*

These values are based on various turning positions and include a safety allowance of 2 mm.

Using a torque wrench

When using a torque wrench, the same values as for using a socket spanner can be assumed provided the following (normal) conditions apply:
• ratchet size of torque wrench < 70 mm
• the same sockets are used

Corrosion risks, corrosivity categories (tab. 1, DIN EN ISO 12944-2)

Corrosivity category and corrosion risk	Loss in thickness* p.a. [µm] Carbon steel	Zinc	Examples of typical environments External	Internal	Required film thickness [µm]	Binder basis of suitable paint
C 1 insignificant	≤ 1.3	≤ 0.1	–	Insulated buildings, I≤ 60% relative humidity		
C 2 low	> 1.3–25	> 0.1–0.7	Low pollution, dry climate, e.g. rural areas	Occasionally heated or uninsulated buildings with occasional condensation, e.g. warehouses, sports halls	K: 80 M: 120 L: 160	AY, CR PUR, AK-PUR AK,
C 3 moderate	> 25–50	> 0.7–2.1	Urban and industrial atmospheres with moderate SO2 pollution, or moderate coastal climate (low salinity)	Interiors with high relative humidity and low pollution, e.g. breweries, laundries, dairies	K: 120 M: 160 L: 200	AK (160 µm), AY (200 µm) PVC PUR, AK-PUR, EP, CR
C 4 severe	> 50–80	> 2.1–4.2	Industrial atmosphere and coastal atmosphere with moderate salinity	Swimming pools, chemical processing plants, boat-houses over seawater	K: 160 M: 200 L: 240–280	PVC PUR EP CR (200 µm)
C 5 very severe I (I = industrial)	> 80–200	> 4.2–8.4	Industrial atmosphere with high relative humidity and aggressive conditions	Buildings or parts thereof with almost constant condensation and severe pollution	M: 280–500 L: 500	PUR, CR, PVC EP, SI with Zn primers offering cathodic protection
C 5 very severe M (M = marine)	> 80–200	> 4.2–8.4	Coastal and offshore areas with high salinity	Buildings or parts thereof with almost constant condensation and severe pollution	M: 240–280 L: 320	CR, PVC, EP, PUR EP, PUR

* Also expressed in terms of a loss in weight [g/m²]
  100 µm = 0.1 mm
Duration of protection to DIN EN ISO 12944-1:
K short: 2–5 years
M medium: 5–15 years
L long: > 15 years

Paint systems for protecting steel structures against corrosion in atmospheric conditions, based on DIN EN ISO 12944-5
Surface preparation: Sa 2½ quality (DIN EN ISO 12944-4) and roughness category Ry5, 40 to < 80 µm (DIN EN ISO 8503-1)

System No.	Factory Priming coat based on...	Reqd. film thk. [µm]	Undercoat or finishing coat based on...	Reqd. film thk. [µm]	No. of coats	Building site Finishing coats	Reqd. film thk. [µm]	No. of coats	System Reqd. film thk. [µm]
1	AK zinc phosphate	100			1–2	AK	60	1	160
2	EP zinc dust	60	AY-Hydro	100	2–3				160
3	EP zinc phosphate	160			1–2				160
4	AK zinc phosphate	100			1–2	AK	100	1–2	200
5	AY-Hydro zinc phosphate	120			1–2	AK, AY, PVC	80	1–2	200
6	EP zinc dust	60	EP, PUR	100	2–3				160
7	EP zinc phosphate	80	EP, PUR	120	2–3				200
8	EP zinc dust	60	AY-Hydro	80	2	AY, PVC	60	1	200
9	EP zinc dust	80	EP, PUR	100	2–3	PUR	60	1	240
10	EP zinc dust	80	AY-Hydro	100	2–3	AY, PVC	60	1	240
11	EP zinc phosphate	160	EP, PUR	120	2–4				280
12	EP zinc dust	80	EP, PUR	160	2–3	PUR	80	1–2	320
13	EP zinc phosphate	80	EP, PUR	160	2–3	PUR	80	1–2	320

Corrosivity category columns: C2 (short, medium, long), C3 (short, medium, long), C4 (short, medium, long), C5-I (short, medium, long), C5-M (short, medium, long)

- Undercoats and finishing coats with or without micaceous iron pigments
- EP finishing coat may be used instead of PUR finishing coat in the case of interior pollution
- EP also includes EP combinations provided equivalence has been verified
- 1-part PUR zinc dust and 1 K/2 K ESI zinc dust may be used instead of EP zinc dust (relative humidity during application and curing ≥ 50 %).
  ESI zinc dust may be used only when a second coat is not applied in the factory or systems with enhanced thermal stability (up to 400 °C) are required.

**Overview of stainless steels with corrosion properties according to general building authority approval Z-30.3-6 dated 5 Dec 2003
(DIN EN 10088 contains further stainless steels)**

No.	Designation	Material No.	Type[1]	Resistance class	Pollution and typical applications for building components and fasteners	as-suppl. condition	welded condition	Possible surface properties using NIROSTA (Thyssen Krupp) as an example
	Steel grade			Corrosion		Resistance to inter-crystalline corrosion in..		
1	X2CrNi12	1.4003	F	I/low	Constructions in interiors apart from wet areas	no	no	1E, 2H, 2B, 2R, 2G
2	X6Cr17	1.4016	F			yes	no	1E, 2H, 2B, 2R, 2G
3	X5CrNi18-10	1.4301	A	II/moderate	Accessible constructions without significant chloride and sulphur dioxide loads, no industrial atmospheres; suitable for internal and external applications	yes	no	1E, 2H, 2B, 2R, 2G
4	X2CrNi18-10	1.4307	A			yes	yes	1E, 2B, 2R, 2G
5	X2CrNiCu18-9-4	1.4567	A			–	–	–
6	X6CrNiTi18-10	1.4541	A			yes	yes	1E, 2B, 2R, 2G
7	X2CrNiN18-7	1.4318	A			yes	yes	1E, 2H, 2B, 2R, 2G
8	X5CrNiMo17-12-2	1.4401	A	III/medium	Constructions with moderate chloride and sulphur dioxide loads, and inaccessible constructions; suitable for industrial atmospheres and coastal areas	yes	no	1E, 2H, 2B, 2R, 2G
9	X2CrNiMo17-12-2	1.4404	A			yes	yes	1E, 2H, 2B, 2R, 2G
10	X3CrNiCuMo17-11-3-2	1.4578	A			–	–	–
11	X6CrNiMoTi17-12-2	1.4571	A			yes	yes	1E, 2B, 2R, 2G
12	X2CrNiMoN17-13-5	1.4439	A			yes	yes	2B, 2R, 2G
13	X2CrNiMoN22-5-3	1.4462	AF	IV/high	High corrosion load due to chlorine and/or chlorides and/or sulphur dioxide and high air humidity, also concentrations of pollutants (e.g. road tunnels)	yes	yes	1E, 2B, 2G
14	X1NiCrMoCu25-20-5	1.4539	A			yes	yes	1E, 2B, 2R, 2G
15	X2CrNiMnMoNbN25-18-5-4	1.4565	A			yes	yes	2B, 2R
16	X1NiCrMoCuN25-20-7	1.4529	A			yes	yes	–
17	X1CrNiMoCuN20-18-7	1.4547	A			yes	yes	–

[1] F = ferritic steel, AF = austenitic-ferritic steel, A = austenitic steel

Typical surface properties of stainless steels (DIN EN 10088-3 & Doc. 960 *Oberflächen im Bauwesen* from ISER, the Rustproof Stainless Stainless Steel Info Centre

Processing	Code	Treatment	Surface properties	Types of product[2]		
				I	II	III
Hot-formed	1U	No heat treatment, no descaling	Covered in mill scale (ground locally if necessary)	×	×	×
	1C	Heat treatment, no descaling	Covered in mill scale (ground locally if necessary)	×	×	×
	1E	Heat treatment, mechanical descaling	Essentially free from mill scale (isolated black patches may be present)	×	×	×
	1D	Heat treatment, pickling	Free from mill scale, few reflections, slightly rough	×	×	–
	1X	Heat treatment, premachined (scraped or pre-twisted)	Metallically clean	–	×	–
Subsequent cold-working	2H	Heat treatment, mechanical or chemical descaling	Smooth and bright, essentially smoother than 1E, 1D or 1X	–	×	–
	2D	Heat treatment, pickling (redrawn)	Smoother than 1E or 1D, matt surface	–	×	–
	2B	Heat treatment, worked (scraped), mechanical burnishing	Smoother and brighter than 1E, 1D or 1X, reflective grey appearance	–	×	–
	2R	Bright annealing under exclusion of air, light re-rolling	High-gloss, reflective surface, extremely smooth	Flat products only		
Special finishing	1G or 2G	Centreless grinding	Consistent finish, type and degree of ground finish to be agreed	–	×	–
	1P or 2P	Polishing	Smoother and brighter than 1G or 2G, reflective high-gloss surface	–	×	–

[2] I = rolled wire, II = bars, sections, III = semi-finished product

Minor imperfections in the surface due to the method of production are permissible. More exact requirements regarding the surface finish must be agreed upon placing an order (see DIN EN 10088-2 cl. 8.6).

Standards and directives (selection)

Technical delivery conditions for rolled products for structural steelwork

DIN EN 10029: Hot-rolled steel plates 3 mm thick or above

DIN EN 10131: Cold-rolled uncoated and zinc or zinc-nickel electrolytically coated low carbon and high yield strength steel flat products for cold forming

DIN 59200: Flat products of steel – Hot-rolled wide flats

DIN 18807: Trapezoidal steel sheeting

DIN EN 508: Roofing products from metal sheet

EN 14509: Self-supporting double-skin metal-faced insulating panels

Important standards and directives for the dimensioning, design and execution of structural steelwork

DIN EN 50164 part 1: Lightning protection components – Requirements for connection components

Eurocode 3 parts 1-1 to 1-7: Design of steel structures

Eurocode 4: Design of composite steel and concrete structures

DIN 4108: Thermal protection and energy economy in buildings

DIN 4109: Sound insulation in buildings

DIN 14509: Self-supporting double-skin metal-faced insulating panels

DIN 18800 parts 1-7: Steel structures, design and construction

DIN 18807 parts 1-3: Trapezoidal sheeting in building

DIN 18335: Contract procedures for building works – Steel construction works

DIN 18338: Contract procedures for building works – Roof covering and roof sealing works

DIN 18339: Contract procedures for building works – Sheet metal works

DIN 18360: Contract procedures for building works – Metal construction works

DASt Guideline 010: Use of high-strength screws in steel construction

DASt Guideline 103: Guidelines on the application of Eurocode 3 (NAD)

DASt Guideline 104: Guidelines on the application of Eurocode 4 (NAD)

DASt Guideline 016: Design and detailing of loadbearing structures of thin-walled cold-formed components

Corrosion protection

DIN EN ISO 1461: Hot-dip galvanized coatings on fabricated iron and steel articles

DIN EN ISO 12944 parts 1-8: Paints and varnishes – Corrosion protection of steel structures by protective paint systems

DIN 55928 parts 1-8: Corrosion protection of steel structures by the application of organic or metallic coatings

Fire protection

DIN 4102 parts 1-4: Fire behaviour of building materials and building components

Eurocode 3 parts 1-2 with DIN Special Report 93 as NAD

DIN 18230: Structural fire protection in industrial buildings

DIN 18234: Fire safety of large roofs for buildings

DASt Guideline 019: Fire protection of steel and composite components in office and administrative buildings

Associations (selection)

Bauen mit Stahl e.V.
Sohnstr. 65
40237 Düsseldorf
Tel.: +49 211 6707828
Fax: +49 211 6707829
zentrale@bauen-mit-stahl.de
www.bauen-mit-stahl.de

Bundesverband Deutscher Stahlhandel e.V.
Max-Plank-Str. 1
40237 Düsseldorf
Tel.: +49 211 864970
Fax: +49 211 8649722
info-bds@stahlhandel.com
www.stahlhandel.com

Bundesverband Korrosionsschutz e.V.
Neuköllner Str. 2
50676 Cologne
Tel.: +49 221 248912
Fax: +49 221 249375
info@bundesverband-korrosionsschutz.de
www.bundesverband-korrosionsschutz.de

Deutscher Ausschuss für Stahlbau, DASt
Sohnstr. 65
40237 Düsseldorf
www.stahlbau-verband.de

DIBt Deutsches Institut f. Bautechnik
Kolonnenstr. 30 L
10829 Berlin
Tel.: +49 30 787730244
Fax: +49 30 78730320
rsm@dibt.de
www.dibt.de

DIN Deutsches Institut f. Normung e.V.
Burggrafenstr. 6
10787 Berlin
Tel.: +49 30 26010
Fax: +49 30 26011260
www.din.de

DSV Deutscher Schraubenverband e.V.
Goldene Pforte 1
58093 Hagen-Emst
Tel.: +49 2331 958849
Fax: +49 2331 51044
www.dsv.wsu.de

Deutscher Stahlbau-Verband DSTV
Sohnstr. 65
40237 Düsseldorf
Tel.: +49 211 6707800
Fax: +49 211 6707820
www.deutscherstahlbau.de

ECCS-CECM-EKS
Av. des Ombrages, bte. 20
1200 Brussels, Belgium
Tel.: +32 2 7620429
Fax: +32 2 7620935
eccs@steelconstruct.com
www.steelconstruct.com

Galileo – Kreatives Bauen mit Sandwich
PO Box 1164
94451 Deggendorf
Tel.: +49 160 94972680
Fax: +49 991 285925
galileo@sandwichbau.de
www.sandwichbau.de

Gütegemeinschaft Stahlhochbau e.V.
RAL-Gütegemeinschaft
www.ggs-stahlbau.de
IFBS Industrieverband für Bausysteme im Stahlleichtbau e.V.
Max-Planck-Straße 4
40237 Düsseldorf
Tel.: +49 211 914270
Fax: +49 211 672034
www.ifbs.de

Industrieverband Feuerverzinken e.V.
Institut Feuerverzinken GmbH
Sohnstraße 70
40237 Düsseldorf
Tel.: +49 211 6907650
Fax: +49 211 689599
www.feuerverzinken.com

Informationsstelle Edelstahl Rostfrei
Sohnstr. 65
40237 Düsseldorf
Tel.: +49 221 6707835
Fax: +49 221 7607344
info@edelstahl-rostfrei.de
www.edelstahl-rostfrei.de

Stahlbau Zentrum Schweiz
Seefeldstr. 25
8034 Zurich, Switzerland
Tel.: +41 44 2618980
Fax: +41 44 2620962
info@szs.ch
www.szs.ch

Stahl-Informations-Zentrum
Sohnstr. 65
40237 Düsseldorf
Tel.: +49 211 6707844
Fax: +49 211 6707344
siz@stahl-info.de
www.stahl-info.de

Steel Construction Institute
Silkwood Park
Ascot, Berkshire SL5 7QN
England
Tel.: +44 1344 623345
Fax: +44 1344 622944
reception@steel-sci.com
www.steel-sci.org

Appendix

Verband der deutschen Lackindustrie e.V.
Karlstr. 21
60329 Frankfurt am Main
Tel.: +49 69 25561411
Fax: +49 69 25561358
vdl@vci.de www.lackindustrie.de

Verein Deutscher Eisenhüttenleute (VDEh)
Information Centre & Library
Sohnstr. 65
40237 Düsseldorf
Tel.: +49 211 914270
Fax: +49 211 672034
reinhard.winkelgrund@stahl-info.de
www.vdeh.de

Österreichischer Stahlbauverband (ÖSTV)
Wiedner Hauptstr. 63
1045 Vienna, Austria
Tel.: +43 1 5039474
Fax: +43 1 5039474227
stahlbau@fmmi.at
www.stahlbauverband.at

British Constructional Steelwork Association
Ltd. (BCSA)
4 Whitehall Court, Westminster
London SW1A 2ES, England
Tel.: +44 20 7839 8566
Fax: +44 20 7976 1634
postroom@steelconstruction.org
www.steelconstruction.org

Manufacturers (selection)

Arcelor Gruppe
Subbelrather Str. 13
50672 Cologne
Tel.: +49 221 5729256
Fax: +49 221 5729285
www.arcelor.com

Corus Bausysteme GmbH (formerly Kalzip)
August-Horch-Str. 20-22
56070 Koblenz
Tel.: +49 261 98340
Fax: +49 261 9834100
kalzip@corusgroup.com
www.corusgroup.com

AG der Dillinger Hüttenwerke
Werkstr. 1
66763 Dillingen/Saar
Tel.: +49 6831 470
Fax: +49 6831 472212
info@dillinger.biz
www.dillinger.de

Bauglasindustrie GmbH
Hüttenstr. 33
66839 Schmelz/Saar
Tel.: +49 6887 30322
Fax: +49 6887 30345
www.pilkington.de

Donges Stahlbau GmbH
Mainzer Str. 55
PO Box 10 04 51
64204 Darmstadt
Tel.: +49 6151 8890
Fax.: +49 6151 889219
www.donges.de

Hoesch Hohenlimburg GmbH
58117 Hagen
Tel.: +49 2334 910
Fax: +49 2334 913369
info.hoesch-hohenlimburg@
thyssenkrupp.com
www.hoesch-hohenlimburg.de

Helling & Neuhaus GmbH & CO. KG
Open-Grid Flooring Division
Gottlieb-Daimler-Str. 2
33334 Gütersloh
Tel.: +49 5241 6040
Fax. +49 5241 60440
gitterroste@seppeler.de
www.gitterroste.de

Jansen AG
Stahlröhrenwerk
9463 Oberriet SG, Switzerland
Tel.: +41 71 7639111
Fax: +41 71 7612270
info@jansen.com
www.jansen.com

Hüttenwerke Krupp Mannesmann GmbH
Ehinger Str. 200
47259 Duisburg-Huckingen
Tel.: +49 203 99901
Fax: +49 203 9994411
post@hkm.de
www.hkm.de

Stahlbau Lamparter
Leipziger Str. 12-18
34260 Kaufungen
Tel.: +49 561 951200
Fax: +49 561 9512088
info@stahlbau-lamparter.de
www.stahlbau-lamparter.de

Opticor Systemberatung (corrosion protection)
Sohnstr. 70
40237 Düsseldorf
Tel.: +49 211 69076529
Fax: +49 211 689599
info@opticor.de
www.opticor.de

Peikko GmbH
Brinker Weg 15
34513 Waldeck
Tel.: +49 5634 1231
Fax: +49 5634 7572
www.peikko.de

Pfeifer Seil- & Hebetechnik GmbH
Dr.-Karl-Lenz-Str. 66
87700 Memmingen
Tel.: +49 8331 9370
Fax: +49 8331 937294
presse@pfeifer.de
www.pfeifer.de

Pilkington Holding GmbH
Alfredstr. 236
45133 Essen
Tel.: +49 201 1254
Fax: +49 201 1255025
www.pilkington.de

Salzgitter AG
Eisenhüttenstr. 99

38239 Salzgitter
Tel.: +49 5341 2101
Fax: +49 5341 212727
info@szmh-group.com
www.salzgitter-ag.de

Schöck Bauteile GmbH
Vimbucher Str. 2
76534 Baden-Baden
Tel.: +49 722 39670
Fax: +49 722 3967450
schoeck@schoeck.de
www.schoeck.de

ThyssenKrupp Hoesch Bausysteme GmbH
Hammerstr. 11
57223 Kreuztal
Tel.: +49 2732 5991599
www.tks-bau.com
ThyssenKrupp Stahl AG
Kaiser-Wilhelm-Str. 100
47166 Duisburg
Tel.: +49 203 521
Fax: +49 203 5225102
www.thyssenkrupp-stahl.com

Vallourec & Mannesmann Tubes
130, rue de Silly
92100 Boulogne, France
Tel.: +33 1 49093919
Fax: +33 1 49093990
www.vmtubes.com

Further reading (selection)

Grundlagen für das Entwerfen und
Konstruieren, Kurt Ackermann,
Karl Krämer Verlag, Stuttgart, 1983

Tragsysteme, Heino Engel,
Deutsche Verlags Anstalt GmbH,
Stuttgart, 2006

Stahlbau im Detail, Friedrich Grimm,
WEKA Baufachverlage GmbH,
Augsburg, 1994

Stahlbau-Brandschutz-Handbuch,
Hass, Meyer-Ottens, Richter,
Ernst & Sohn Verlag, Berlin, 1994

Der Entwurf von Tragwerken,
Führer, Ingendaaij, Stein,
Verlag Rudolf Müller, Cologne, 1995

Stahlbau, Petersen,
Vieweg & Sohn Verlagsgesellschaft mbH,
Braunschweig/Wiesbaden, 1993

Steel Construction Manual,
Schulitz, Sobek, Habermann,
Birkhäuser Verlag, Basel/Institut für internationale
Architektur-Dokumentation, Munich, 2000

Stahlbauatlas,
Schulitz, Sobek, Habermann,
Birkhäuser Verlag, Basel/Institut für internatio-
nale Architektur-Dokumentation, Munich 1999

Stahlbau Handbuch, vol. 1 & 2,
Verlag Stahlbau-Verlagsgesellschaft mbH,
Cologne, 2002

Stahl im Hochbau, Anwenderhandbuch,
Verlag Stahleisen GmbH, Düsseldorf, 1969

Typisierte Anschlüsse im Stahlhochbau,
vol. 1 & 2, Deutscher Stahlbau-Verband DSTV,
Stahlbau-Verlagsgesellschaft mbH

Ausführung von Stahlbauten,
Erläuterungen zu DIN 18800-7,
Beuth Verlag GmbH, Berlin, 2005

Stahlbau-Profile, Verlag Stahleisen GmbH,
Düsseldorf, 2004

Stahlbau Kalender (published annually),
Ernst & Sohn Verlag, Berlin

DIN Handbooks Nos 10, 140 & 193, Fasteners,
Beuth Verlag GmbH, Berlin, 2001/2006/2005

DIN Handbook No. 69, Stahlhochbau,
Beuth Verlag GmbH, Berlin 2005

Stahlbau I+II, Thiele, Lohse,
Verlag B.G. Teubner, Stuttgart, 1997/2000

Steel Buildings, pub. No. 35/03,
BCSA, London, 2003

Index

Picture credits

The authors and publishers would like to express their sincere gratitude to all those who have assisted in the production of this book, be it through providing photos or artwork or granting permission to reproduce their documents or providing other information. All the drawings in this book were specially commissioned. Photographs not specifically credited were taken by the architects or are works photographs or were supplied from the archives of the magazine DETAIL. Despite intensive endeavours we were unable to establish copyright ownership in just a few cases; however, copyright is assured. Please notify us accordingly in such instances.

The authors and publishers would also like to thank Stahlbau Donges, Darmstadt, for their technical advice and assistance in compiling the artwork for this book.
And thanks also go to Saarstahl AG, Völklingen, and Arcelor, Cologne, for the provision of artwork.

page 30, 36:
Alexander Reichel, Kassel

page 31:
Schweißtechnische Lehr- und Versuchsanstalt, Munich

page 35 top left:
SOM Architekten, Chicago

page 38 top centre:
Christoph Kraneburg, Cologne

page 40, 90, 91:
Alexander Felix, Munich

page 41 top centre:
David Hirsch, New York/Montreal

page 41 bottom right:
Kauffmann Theilig & Partner,
Ostfildern/Kemnat

page 42:
Christina Schulz, Munich

page 43 top centre:
Unger Stahlbau GmbH, Oberwart

page 46 top centre:
Sigrid Neubert, Dresden

page 47:
SLV, Munich

page 48 top centre:
Balthazar Korab, Montreal

page 49 top left:
Jo Reid, John Peck, Newport

page 49 top centre:
Alastair Hunter

page 50 top right, 92:
Frank Kaltenbach, Munich

page 51 top left:
Klaus Frahm/artur, Essen

page 51 top right:
Michel Denancé, Paris

page 52 top centre:
Hedrich Blessing, Chicago

page 53 top left:
Timothy Soar, London

page 54 top left, 58, 60, 61:
Dietmar Strauss, Besingheim

page 54 top right:
Klemens Ortmeyer, Braunschweig

page 56 bottom, 62, 63 bottom right:
Richie Müller, Munich

page 63 top right, 98, 99:
Jens Weber, Munich

page 65:
Salzgitter AG

page 69 centre:
Ras Reinhard Maschinenbau GmbH,
Sindelfingen

page 70 top left:
Stappert Spezial-Stahl Handel GmbH,
Düsseldorf

page 70 top centre:
ThyssenKrupp Stahl AG, Duisburg

page 70 top right:
Fachabteilung f. Lochbleche im Industrieverband Stahlverarbeitung e.V., Siegen

page 71, 72 top centre:
Hoesch-Siegerlandwerke GmbH, Siegen

page 72 top left:
ThyssenKrupp Nirosta GmbH, Krefeld

page 73 top left:
Helling & Neuhaus GmbH & Co. KG,
open-grid flooring division, Gütersloh

page 73 top centre:
Meiser Gitterroste, Oelsnitz

page 74 top left & top centre:
Heike Werner, Munich

page 74 top right:
Uwe Schneider, Völkling

page 75 top left & top right:
Haver & Boecker, Oelde

page 75 top centre:
Holger Lorenz, Dortmund

page 75 bottom left:
Gebrüder Kufferath AG, Düren

page 75 bottom centre & bottom right:
DOH Drahterzeugnisse, Solms-Oberndorf

page 76, 77:
Pfeiffer Seil- & Hebetechnik GmbH,
Memmingen

page 80 top left:
PSE Redaktionsservice GmbH,
Stefan Elgaß, Geretsried

page 80 top centre:
Otto Suhner GmbH, Bad Säckingen

page 81 top left:
ThyssenKrupp Xervon GmbH,
Gelsenkirchen

page 81 top right, 83:
Caparol Farben & Lacke, Ober-Ramstadt

page 84:
Hensel GmbH, Bornsen

page 85:
Schöck Bauteile GmbH,
Baden-Baden/Steinach

page 88:
Werner Huthmacher, Berlin

page 93:
Christian Kandzia, Stuttgart

page 96:
Roland Halbe/artur, Essen

page 10, 101:
Adolf Bereuther, Lauterach (A)

page 102, 103:
Norbert Miguletz, Frankfurt am Main

Full-page plates

page 6:
Donges Stahlbau, Darmstadt

page 30:
Alexander Reichel, Kassel

page 44:
Richie Müller, Munich

page 64:
Donges Stahlbau, Darmstadt

page 78:
Norbert Miguletz, Frankfurt am Main

page 86:
Roland Halbe/artur, Essen

page 104:
Johannes Marburg, Berlin